A History of Torture
in Britain

A History of Torture in Britain

Simon Webb

PEN & SWORD
HISTORY
AN IMPRINT OF PEN & SWORD BOOKS LTD.
YORKSHIRE – PHILADELPHIA

First published in Great Britain in 2018 by
Pen & Sword History
An imprint of
Pen & Sword Books Ltd
Yorkshire - Philadelphia

Hardback ISBN: 978 1 52671 929 4
Paperback ISBN: 978 1 52675 148 5

A CIP catalogue record for this book is
available from the British Library.

Printed and bound in England
By TJ International Ltd, Padstow, Cornwall.

Pen & Sword Books Ltd incorporates the Imprints of Pen & Sword Books Archae-
ology, Atlas, Aviation, Battleground, Discovery, Family History, History, Maritime,
Military, Naval, Politics, Railways, Select, Transport, True Crime, Fiction, Frontline
Books, Leo Cooper, Praetorian Press, Seaforth Publishing, Wharncliffe and White
Owl.

For a complete list of Pen & Sword titles please contact

PEN & SWORD BOOKS LIMITED
47 Church Street, Barnsley, South Yorkshire, S70 2AS, England
E-mail: enquiries@pen-and-sword.co.uk
Website: www.pen-and-sword.co.uk

or

PEN AND SWORD BOOKS
1950 Lawrence Rd, Havertown, PA 19083, USA
E-mail: Uspen-and-sword@casematepublishers.com
Website: www.penandswordbooks.com

Contents

List of Illustrations

1. The public mutilation and branding with red-hot irons of a blasphemer during the rule of Oliver Cromwell.

2. Libelling the monarch in Elizabethan England could result in having the right hand chopped off.

3. A contemporary drawing of the origin of torture in Britain; a reluctant suspect is handed a red-hot iron bar, which he must carry for nine paces.

4. Calling upon God to decide innocence or guilt; the ordeal by cold water.

5. The subject of 1,000 cartoons.

6. Being married to the Duke of Exeter's daughter; the rack in action in the Tower of London.

7. Skeffington's Gyves, otherwise known as the Scavenger's Daughter; the opposite procedure to the rack, it squashed, rather than stretched, the victim.

8. Breaking on the wheel was a brutal death. It was occasionally inflicted in Scotland, but never in England.

9. Although never popular in England, thumbscrews were used in Scotland under a variety of names, such pilliwinks.

10. The *peine forte et dure* in action; a torture which was used in Britain well into the eighteenth century on those who refused to enter a plea when brought to trial.

11. Matthew Hopkins, the self-styled 'Witchfinder General'; a man who was ready and willing to use torture in pursuit of the Devil's agents.

12. Slaves in British colonies were treated like cattle, being branded and whipped at the will of their 'owners'.

13. Gibbetting alive (hanging a man in chains to die of exposure and thirst), was used in both England and the Caribbean.

14. Luisa Calderon was a 15 year-old girl tortured at the orders of the British general, Thomas Picton.

Introduction

Torture is the practice of inflicting severe pain on people, either to punish them or persuade them to say or do something. Perhaps the most succinct and accurate definition of torture is still that given by Dr Johnson in his famous dictionary, which was first published in 1755. In it, he described torture as being, 'pain by which guilt is punished or confession extorted'. Torture may be conducted as either a private enterprise or judicially, on behalf of the state. In this book, we shall be looking at the 'official' use of torture, sanctioned by the Crown, courts, police, army or other legal authorities in Britain and its possessions overseas. Before going any further, it might be as well to deal briefly with a widespread myth to the effect that torture has been unlawful in Britain since 1215, when it was expressly forbidden by Magna Carta. So common is this misapprehension that the matter will be dealt with in some detail in Chapter 2. For now, it is enough to say that the idea of torture being extra-judicial or outside the law of England, was not devised until the early seventeenth century, over 400 years after the drafting of Magna Carta.

Perhaps the best way to expose the mistaken notion that torture has only been practised in Britain to a limited extent and in a hole-and-corner way, in dark dungeons out of the public view, is to give some contemporary accounts of its use. The following passage, taken from *The London Journal* of 12 June 1731, just as the Enlightenment was gaining pace in Europe, tells of the punishment inflicted on the aptly named Japhet Crook.

Posing as 'Sir Peter Stringer', the elderly Crook forged documents suggesting that he owned a tract of land in Essex. He then raised a mortgage on the land. Japhet Crook was 70 years of age at this time and had carried out similar frauds for years without being caught. This time though, his luck ran out. He was arrested and brought to trial. The sentence was one of life imprisonment, but before that he was ordered to undergo public punishment. On 9 June 1731, Crook was brought from prison and set in the pillory at London's Charing Cross. *The London Journal* relates what happened next:

> He stood an hour thereon, after which a chair was set upon the pillory and he being put therein, the hangman with a sort of pruning knife, cut off both his ears and immediately a surgeon clapt a styptic thereon. The

executioner, with a pair of scissors, cut the left nostril until it was near quite through and afterwards cut the right nostril at once. He bore all this with great patience, but when in pursuance of his sentence, the right nostril was seared with a red-hot iron, he was in such violent pain that his left nostril was let alone.

Ears cut off, nostrils slit with scissors, red-hot irons; it is difficult to know what word one could possibly apply to such horrors, other than 'torture'. Using red-hot irons on people's faces was a not uncommon punishment in Britain for centuries, along with mutilations, up to and including the amputation of hands and feet. One or two more examples might underline the point. In December 1655, during the time that Oliver Cromwell ruled the country, a Quaker called James Naylor fell foul of the authorities and was convicted of blasphemy. An eyewitness describes what was done to this man, whose only offence was to preach the Gospel, after he had been set in the pillory at the Royal Exchange in London;

He having stood till two, the executioner took him out, and having bound his arms with cords to the pillory, and he having put forth his tongue, which he freely did, the executioner, with a red-hot iron about the bigness of a quill, bored the same, and by order of the sheriff held it in a small place, to the end that the beholders might see and bear witness that the sentence was thoroughly executed: then having taken it out and pulled the cap off that covered his face, he put a handkerchief over his eyes, and putting his left hand to the back part of his head, and taking the red-hot iron letter in his other hand, put it to his forehead till it smoked . . .

The 'red-hot iron letter' was a 'B' for 'Blasphemer'. This then was the sort of thing one was likely to suffer for holding heterodox religious beliefs during the Commonwealth. This terrible sentence may be seen being executed in Illustration 1.

Two more instances should be sufficient to show that torture was used not merely for publicly for punishment, but also to extract confessions in private. In 1546 a woman called Anne Askew was being imprisoned in London for her unorthodox religious beliefs. Unfortunately, it was the final year of Henry VIII's reign and some people wanted to see his wife Catherine brought down. One way of doing this was to gather evidence that she was a heretic. A woman who, it was thought, might be able to supply information about the queen's heretical leanings was a devout Protestant. Anne Askew was taken to the Tower of London and tortured so severely on the rack that her arms and legs were torn from their sockets. So badly dislocated were her limbs, that she never walked again. (Not that this proved a long-lasting handicap; she was burned at the stake a few weeks later.) There was nothing remarkable about somebody being racked in this way; it could be done by either a royal warrant or an order from the Privy Council. In the century following Anne Askew's torture, a little over eighty warrants were issued for torture by the Tower of London's rack.

It is true, however, that most torture carried out in England was intended as punishment, rather than for the purpose of obtaining information. Very often, as in the two first examples at which we looked, such public exhibitions involved mutilation and the use of red-hot irons. In 1581, a man called John Stubs was unwise enough to write a pamphlet which could have been seen as an attack on Elizabeth I. It was printed by William Pace and in due course, both men found themselves in court. The law was quite clear, that those who insulted the monarch in this way were liable to lose their hands for it. On a scaffold in Westminster, both John Stubs and William Pace had their right hands removed by the simple expedient of placing a butcher's cleaver over the wrist and striking it very hard with a mallet. The stump was then cauterized with a red-hot iron. An example of how this sort of mutilation was carried out may be seen in Illustration 2.

The truth is that torture is as British as cricket or crumpets. It was used from the country's earliest recorded history, both as punishment and also to compel suspected criminals to speak, and its use continued well into the modern period. As late as 1976, the European Court of Human Rights ruled that Britain had been torturing suspects in Northern Ireland. This is no mere historical curiosity!

In the first chapter, we shall examine the origin of the use of torture in England and see how it was used, particularly in the interrogation of those suspected of religious dissent or treason. Mention of torture in this country automatically summons up images of the rack and it is interesting to note that this archetypal instrument of English torture was in use for only a century or so, and that only one rack was operating in the whole country during that time.

Chapter 1

The Use of Torture for Interrogation in Medieval and Tudor England

In the Introduction, we looked at the two different types of judicial torture, that used to extract information and the kind designed simply to inflict pain upon the victim as punishment. Both were being used in the British Isles as far back as recorded history stretches. To explore this idea further, we must, for a short while, abandon our use of the word 'torture' and consider the actual nature of the activity, regardless of what name may be used to describe it. Let us look first at the notion of inflicting severe pain on a suspect as a method of uncovering the truth about a supposed crime, what most people today mean when they talk of 'torture'.

The practice of using an 'ordeal' to establish the innocence or guilt of an accused person was widely used in Britain from the Anglo-Saxon period onwards. By the time of the Norman Conquest, this was the accepted method used to investigate crime and bring perpetrators to justice. The Church was inextricably linked with the practice of trial by ordeal, which meant by implication that it was sanctioned by God himself. The custom of the ordeal was prescribed by law and in many, perhaps most, cases, was the only way of finding out if somebody had committed a crime. Without a police force, unless the criminal was actually caught in the act it was all but impossible to pin the crime on a suspect after the event. The ordeal was essentially a religious process, the discovery of truth by divine revelation, rather than by the examination of evidence.

A century after the invasion of England by William the Conqueror, the ordeal was codified in the Assize of Clarendon, which was an attempt by Henry II to bring all the laws of England into one unified and recognized framework. The Assize of Clarendon was a meeting over which Henry II presided in 1166 and it was held at the royal hunting lodge at Clarendon Palace in Wiltshire. The intention was to create a legal system for England which was to be brought under the king's control, thus limiting the power of the barons in the process. The idea was to discourage any of the barons from imposing their own ideas of law and order and to acknowledge the supremacy of the king and his laws. One section of the Assize of Clarendon talked of how to deal with, '. . . any man who is accused or believed to be a robber, murderer, thief or receiver of robbers or thieves since the King's succession'. It went on to say that, 'Those thus identified shall be put to the ordeal of water . . .' At roughly the same time, Ranulph de Glanvill produced his monumental work on the law of England, *Tractatus de legibus et consuetudinibus regni Anglie*, which translates roughly as 'The Treatise on the Laws and Customs of the Kingdom of England'. He described how a suspected criminal must be, 'made to purge himself by ordeal'.

What were these ordeals which were used to determine the innocence or guilt of those accused of robbery, murder and so on? Three types of ordeal had been in use for centuries and were by 1166 an integral part of the English judicial process. These were the ordeal by cold water, ordeal by hot water and the ordeal by hot iron. All were injurious to the victims and could even result in death.

The ordeal by hot iron was perhaps the most painful and harmful of the three methods. It entailed the suspected criminal being made either to walk nine paces holding a red-hot iron bar or to walk blindfolded and barefoot across nine red-hot iron ploughshares, laid on the floor of the church. Illustration 3 shows a man being handed a red-hot iron bar. He is being supported and will be helped to take nine strides across the floor of the church. We remember once more, the claim that English law has never countenanced the use of torture! By any definition, making somebody hold a piece of red-hot metal or place their feet on it would surely count as torture. A historical instance of how the ordeal by hot iron worked in practice may be of interest.

Edward the Confessor was the penultimate Anglo-Saxon king of England, ruling from 1044 to 1066. According to tradition, his mother Emma of Normandy, the former Queen of England, was accused of having an affair with the Bishop of Winchester. To establish her innocence or guilt, she was compelled to undergo the ordeal of hot iron. Nine flat blades from ploughs, each about the size of a modern-day laptop computer, were made red-hot in a brazier and laid on the floor of the nave of Winchester Cathedral. The former queen was blindfolded and then forced to walk over the hot pieces of iron. Legend has it that after she had completed the ordeal, Emma asked if they would soon reach the red-hot ploughshares. She had not even noticed walking over them and her feet were quite unharmed. This proved her innocence of the accusation made against her.

This then was the essence of trial by ordeal, that God would protect the innocent from harm. For most of those undergoing the ordeal by hot iron or hot water the results would not have been so clear-cut and obvious as they were when Emma of Normandy was put to the test. The usual procedure was that after the person had held or walked on the red-hot iron, the affected area would be bandaged and then examined three days later in the presence of a priest, who would be the final arbiter. If the wound was discoloured or oozing pus, then it meant that God had not acted to protect the person subject to the ordeal. If, on the other hand, the burns or scalds were healing well and the flesh looked healthy, then this was a sign of grace, that the Lord was showing that the individual concerned had been telling the truth.

The ordeal of hot water entailed heating a pot of water, or sometimes oil, until it was boiling and then requiring the accused person to plunge in his or her hand and retrieve a stone or other object which lay at the bottom of the pot. For less serious offences, the arm would only have to be immersed up to the wrist, but for cases of robbery or murder, a deeper vessel was used, which required the person to reach into the boiling liquid until the whole arm up to the elbow was scalded. Sometimes, the pain was such that the stone could not be picked up. In those cases, the ordeal had to be repeated until this was achieved.

Those faced with the ordeal could of course refuse to take part, but this was regarded as being tantamount to an admission of guilt and might consequently result in immediate execution for whatever crime was being investigated. There was also the possibility of confessing and admitting the offence. Honestly and penitence of this kind might lead to a reduced sentence. The ordeal was really no more than a session of torture, designed to discover the truth about an alleged crime.

The final type of ordeal was that of cold water. This entailed the accused being tied up and dropped into a body of cold water such as a pond or lake. The guilty person would be rejected by the water and so float; the innocent would sink and then be rescued and acquitted of the charge against them. We shall look more closely at this ordeal in Chapter 3, when we examine the activities of Matthew Hopkins, the so-called 'Witchfinder General'. We can see a woman being put to the ordeal of cold water in Illustration 4.

There were several problems with the trial by ordeal. One was that judging if a burn or scald was healing well was a purely subjective matter and a priest could be mistaken or even bribed. It also left the administration of justice in the hands of the Church, rather than the Crown, something which monarchs found a little irksome at times. Other difficulties with judging innocence or guilt in this way included the disconcerting, but irrefutable, fact that it ran counter to Scripture. There are a number of Biblical prohibitions against enlisting the aid of the Deity in determining innocence or guilt in this way. The Old Testament book of Deuteronomy, for instance, advises that, 'You shall not put the LORD your God to the test', an injunction repeated by Jesus. These reservations led in 1215 to the Pope forbidding priests from taking any further part in trials by ordeal. That this prohibition came in the same year that King John set his seal to Magna Carta has led to some confusion, in that it has been thought that the abolition of trial by ordeal was somehow associated with Magna Carta. It was not.

It was abandoning the traditional ordeal as a method for deciding guilt which led subsequently to the extensive use of torture in Europe to force confessions from those accused of crimes. This was due to a fundamental difference in the legal systems of England and other countries in Europe. Throughout most of Europe, conviction for a crime could only, by tradition, happen if there were either two eyewitnesses to the crime or a confession by the perpetrator. Circumstantial evidence was judged to be insufficient. Since few murderers are careless enough to kill their victims while people are watching and most will not shrink at perjury after having committed murder, without torture to force a confession, criminals in mainland Europe would have been unlikely ever to be convicted of anything at all.

In England, circumstantial evidence and the word of witnesses about the character of the accused person were all admissible in court. It was for this reason, rather than any delicacy and squeamishness on the part of the English at that time, that torture was not routinely used as an aid in law enforcement the way that it was in France and Germany, for instance. There was another reason to use torture sparingly and this was a practical point which the English grasped, but which was perhaps neglected in most of continental Europe. Over 2,000 years ago, during the time of the Roman Empire, it was known by thoughtful people that torture was not a very efficient way of establishing the truth. Both Cicero and Tacitus observed that torture was just as likely to bring forth falsehood as it was truth. People will say literally anything to avoid extreme pain. They are especially likely to say what the questioner wishes to hear.

Modern research in the fields of trauma and neuroscience confirm precisely what was said by those writers of classical antiquity, about torture being as likely to produce fantasy and lies as it is to reveal the truth. Suffering and stress, the very things which torture is designed to produce, distort perception, disrupt the process of coherent and orderly thinking and cause the subject to generate unreliable narratives and false memories. The more severe the pain and the more prolonged the ordeal, the less likely are the statements wrung from the individual to be accurate and veridical.

In Scotland, where torture was always far more freely used than it was in England, this tendency was very noticeable. An instance of its use in that country will illustrate why evidence obtained in this way is all too often completely worthless. In November 1589, King James VI of Scotland, later to be James I of England, was hoping to sail to Norway to meet up with the 16–year-old girl whom he was scheduled to marry. Unfortunately, the North Sea can be stormy and rough at that time of year and twice he was forced to postpone the crossing. The king got it into his head that the inclement weather must be caused by witchcraft and when he returned to his own country, he started an investigation. More than that, he personally supervised the torture of those accused of causing the foul weather.

One of the first people to be arrested was Agnes Sampson and she naturally denied all knowledge of causing the North Sea to be choppy. The Scots had always been keener on and more ingenious in their use of torture than the English. A rope was twisted round Agnes Sampson's head and then twisted very tight. This is a most agonising experience and she soon changed her tune and began desperately trying to find things to say which would stop any further torture. One of the first things she admitted to was causing a storm at sea, but this was not sufficient. She said to the king, who was present during her torment, 'It was me who called the maelstrom to your ship after your marriage. I cast a cat into the sea with parts of a dead body to raise a storm.'

This was a promising beginning, but those interrogating her knew that there must be more to it than that. They turned the rope around her head even tighter, until Agnes Sampson was almost incoherent with pain. Then she came up with an even better story and said, 'One All Hallow's Eve myself and two hundred other witches went to sea. We sailed up the Firth from North Berwick to Leith in a magic sieve.' This was more like it and after a few similar statements, the torture was stopped. Agnes Sampson was subsequently burned at the stake for witchcraft. This then, is a classic case of torture bringing forth not truth but merely lies. Even the most credulous of readers will perhaps not be able to believe that 201 witches really did sail along the Scottish coast in a sieve! As a means of establishing the truth, torture is all but useless.

From 1219, when the use of ordeal was wholly abandoned in England, trial by jury became the usual way of investigating or trying a suspected crime. It would be rash to assert that torture was never used, but it was viewed a little askance. This was because while not forbidden by either Common Law or Statute, neither was it sanctioned. It was what we would today, describe as being a 'grey area'. On the Continent, most countries had laws relating to the use of torture to obtain confessions. The whole procedure was set out in detail and prescribed by law. Those undertaking the torture of suspected criminals knew that they were following the country's due legal process. England had nothing of the sort. Torture was not forbidden by the law, by neither was it expressly permitted. It is this ambiguity which allowed later jurists to claim that torture was inimical and incompatible with English law. When the eminent lawyer Sir Edward Coke, formerly Attorney General and Speaker of the House of Commons, wrote in the early seventeenth century that, 'there is no law to warrant tortures in this land', the hint was plainly that the practice was opposed by or outside the law. In fact, the law was silent on the point. There may have been no law to warrant torture, but neither was there a law to forbid it.

This ambiguity led to a curious situation in England. Because it was not prescribed by law, those ordered to undertake torture had an understandable fear that they might themselves be acting outside the law when administering torture to a suspect in order to force a confession. This reluctance was overcome by the practice of issuing warrants by the Privy Council or directly from the monarch, ordering that torture be applied. Because the Tudor kings and queens, as well as the first two Stuarts, believed that they were above the law and that it did not apply to them, they thought that their royal prerogative could be extended to those carrying out dubious acts on their behalf. The warrants authorizing torture were therefore issued like guarantees, assuring those operating the rack that they could do so with impunity from any legal consequences. In the century between 1540 and 1640, eighty-one such warrants were made out, indicating that the torture of suspects was rare, but not freakishly so. Roughly every eighteen months during that period, some unfortunate soul was being racked or otherwise mistreated in the Tower of London. Almost all the warrants were for torture to take place in London, mostly at the Tower.

In the centuries following the abolition of trial by ordeal, various means were used in England to encourage prisoners to speak. Torture as such was in general avoided, although some of the methods used were certainly designed to create extreme discomfort. 'Pinching' was one way of encouraging a recalcitrant suspect to talk. A prisoner would be left in his cell with no food and only sufficient water to sustain life. After a period of starvation, many people were only too happy to open up a little in return for a square meal! In the Tower of London, another way of persuading men to be a little more amenable was confinement in a cell known as 'Little Ease'. This was a space no bigger than a cupboard, which was so designed that it was impossible either to sit, stand or lie down in it. A few days in Little Ease worked wonders on even the most obdurate suspect.

Sometimes, the deprivation of food was used in a more systematic and determined way to force victims to do or say something which the interrogators wished to hear. This happened with the so-called 'Carthusian Martyrs' in 1537, three years after Henry VIII had declared himself to be the supreme head of the Church of England. Once he had split from Rome, as part of the process which became known as the Reformation, Henry demanded that all priests and monks acknowledged him as their religious, as well as secular, leader. Those who chose to adhere to the teachings of the Roman Catholic Church and refused to take an oath to this effect were, at least in the eyes of the law, traitors to the Crown.

Slowly but surely, King Henry's agents moved in on the monasteries. These places were thought, quite rightly in some cases, to be hotbeds of opposition to the Reformation. The Carthusian order of monks, who had a monastery at Charterhouse in London, the remains of which may still be seen, were important to Henry. They had a reputation for sanctity and abstinence and having them both acknowledge the king's marriage to Anne Boleyn and also to accept him as their religious leader meant a lot to Henry. It was not to be. The Carthusians were adamant that the Pope was their only true authority, although many monks were prepared to agree that Henry VIII was the rightful temporal ruler of the country. This was not enough and between 1535 and 1537, eighteen members of the order died as a result of their refusal to cooperate with Henry's demands. One of these was that the monks signed the Oath of Succession, acknowledging Anne Boleyn's children as the rightful heirs to the throne. Since Henry's marriage to Anne was undertaken following his divorce from Catherine of Aragon, no devout Catholic could accept this proposition. This infuriated the king, because it was tantamount to declaring that any children Anne had would be illegitimate.

The first to suffer for this defiance were the Prior of Charterhouse and two other high-ranking monks. On 4 May 1535, they were executed for treason by means of being hanged, drawn and quartered, a protracted and agonising death which involved being mutilated and having one's heart cut out. A week later, two leading members of the London Carthusians who had been taken to the north to be tried for treason were also executed. There had been a good deal of unrest in the north, culminating in the Pilgrimage of Grace, which must have looked to Henry VIII a bit like the beginnings of a Catholic uprising. He intended to show the Catholics in Yorkshire that he was in charge and that those who opposed him could expect no mercy. John Rochester and James Walworth were executed in a particularly dreadful way, being, in effect, gibbeted alive. On 11 May 1537 they were hung in chains from York's city wall and left to die of exposure and thirst. Even when dead, their bodies were left hanging from the wall, until they literally fell to pieces.

Two weeks later, three monks from the Charterhouse who also refused to acknowledge the legitimacy of Henry's marriage to Anne Boleyn were arrested and taken to the Marshalsea Prison. On 25 May, Sebastian Newdigate, Humphrey Middlemore and William Exmew were installed in the Marshalsea. All three were chained upright to posts in a most uncomfortable position. Iron rings were fastened around their necks, wrists and ankles and orders were given that they were to receive just enough food and water to prevent them from dying and that they were to be left there, chained to the posts, until they changed their minds about taking the Oath of Succession.

One of the three monks sent to the Marshalsea, Sebastian Newdigate, had been an acquaintance of King Henry's before entering the monastery and there is a legend that the king visited him twice, pleading with him to save his life by taking the oath. This then was a fine form of torture. The prisoners could not sit and the only sleep they could snatch was by leaning against the posts to which they were secured and hoping that they would not fall into too deep a slumber, slipping down and choking to death. They were virtually starving to death as well. All they needed to do was sign a piece of paper and they would be freed at once. None of the three monks would cooperate and after spending fourteen days and nights standing upright on a starvation diet, they were taken to court, where they were all condemned to death for treason. On 19 June 1537, they were dragged to Tyburn on hurdles and then hanged, drawn and quartered.

The final group of the men who became known as the Carthusian Martyrs were arrested on 18 May. Of the twenty-eight members who were seized, eighteen agreed to sign the Oath of Succession. The rest were taken to Newgate gaol, where they were treated in the same way as the three who had been held in the Marshalsea prison. The ten of them were chained upright to posts and left to reflect upon their refusal to acknowledge Henry as both their temporal and spiritual leader. It is unclear whether the torture of this group was undertaken with the same purpose as that of the three men who had earlier been imprisoned under similar conditions, that is to say, if the king hoped that they would change their mind and sign the oath or if, on the other hand, it was just a way of executing them privately. Whatever the aim, there were those who sort to frustrate it. A devout Catholic woman called Margaret Clements now enters the picture. She was very well connected, having been brought up in the home of Sir Thomas More, who was a distant relative. Margaret Clements felt that the Lord was urging her to save the lives of the Carthusians being held in Newgate and for this purpose she enlisted the help of some of the jailers there.

The men chained to the posts were allowed water, but no food and so Margaret Clements bribed her way into the prison, disguised as a milkmaid, carrying bread and meat in her milk-can. This she fed to the starving prisoners. She also tried to help clean them up a little, as there was of course no sanitary provision for people in their position. Unfortunately, the king maintained a personal interest in the Carthusians and after a week, enquired if any of them had yet died. The jailer became too frightened to allow Margaret Clements into the prison again, but she was permitted to climb onto the roof, remove some slates and dangle pieces of meat down for the men. This too was stopped after a while and the men simply died of exhaustion and hunger. None had any intention of giving in to the demand to sign the Oath of Succession and so they were allowed to die. Throughout June and July, all but three died. Richard Bere lasted until 9 August and Thomas Johnson did not die until 20 September. He had spent over four months, chained upright and starving almost the entire time. A worse form of torture is hard to imagine.

Perhaps the commonest way of establishing a fruitful dialogue with a suspect during the reign of the Tudors was to suspend him from the wall by his manacled hands. This image, of the half-starved prisoner hanging from the wall of a dungeon, is of course a cliched one and the subject of any number of cartoons. The reality though was that hanging by the wrists in this way was, after several hours, agonising and could even result in permanent disability. In 1595 a Catholic priest called Henry Walpole was subjected to the manacles for so long that his hands were permanently maimed. In Illustration 5 we see an unfortunate prisoner being subjected to the manacles. In this instance, questioning is taking place as he hangs, suspended by his wrists.

The manacles were often effective, but time-consuming. By the middle of the fifteenth century, it was felt that something a little speedier was needed. Harsh questioning and torture were not used in ordinary criminal cases, but only where conspiracies against the state were suspected. It was thought to be imperative that information about plots to overthrow the king or queen were thoroughly and swiftly investigated and when one suspect was detained, then it was a race against time to catch others before they realized that they were in danger. For this reason, in 1447 the first rack ever seen in England was installed in the Tower of London.

The rack is one of the most ancient machines devised to inflict pain on people, having been in use since at least the fifth century BC. We know this, because the Greek playwright Aristophanes, writing at that time, mentions the rack in his play *The Frogs*. Conversation between two of the characters, Aiakos and Xanthias, turns to torture and Xanthias says, 'Any way you like. Rack, thumbscrews, whip. Bricks on the chest, vinegar up the nose – anything.' The origin of the rack is more ancient than this though. The legend of Theseus tells of the villainous Procrustes who kept a house where travellers were invited to try the bed. If they were too long for it, he lopped off their feet to make them fit, but if, on the other hand, they were too short, he used a rack to stretch them to the correct size.

In 1447, England was about to be swept by the civil war known as the Wars of the Roses. The descent into chaos was hardly helped by the weak and mentally unstable Henry VI. Conspiracies and plots abounded and so it was thought that it might not be a bad idea to be able to question those arrested for treason more effectively. In the summer of 1447 John Holland, Duke of Exeter and Constable of the Tower, procured a rack to use for questioning suspected traitors. It became known informally, for this reason, as 'The Duke of Exeter's Daughter'! Being stretched on the rack was sometimes referred to facetiously as being 'married to the Duke of Exeter's daughter'.

The rack causes extreme pain and a session with it can result in irreparable damage to the body. A rack may be seen in Illustration 6. It is simple enough, just a stout frame of oak, with rollers at each end, which can be turned with levers. Ropes are attached to these rollers, two on each, and these are fastened around the ankles and wrists of the victim. Then, the stretching begins.

At first, the pain is chiefly in the long muscles of the arms and legs. Then, the stomach muscles also begin to feel the strain. As the tension increases, some ligaments tear loose, with agonising consequences for the man being slowly torn apart. The muscles in the arm are the weakest and are the first to be damaged, followed by those in the legs and then the sheet of muscles covering the abdomen.

The pain by this time, as the fibres of the muscles are snapped or wrenched free of their moorings, is excruciating, but it is not the worst. That is yet to come.

Once the muscles give way, the full strain is taken by the joints of the arms and legs. Slowly, but inexorably, the arms are pulled from their sockets in the shoulders. Then the legs too are dislocated, torn from the hips. Anybody who has ever dislocated their shoulder will know the sickening pain which such an injury entails. The agony of having both arms and legs dislocated simultaneously is almost inconceivable. Even that was not the end though, because if the torture was maintained further, then the elbows and knees too would be drawn apart, leaving the victim a helpless cripple. We know this from the accounts of one of those who suffered this torment, the only woman ever to be racked in England.

Anne Askew was born in Lincolnshire in 1521. Her family were well-to-do and arranged for her marriage to a wealthy landowner. Her husband was a fervent Catholic, but Anne was already having doubts about certain aspects of Catholic doctrine such as transubstantiation, the belief that the wafer of the host actually becomes transformed into the body of Christ, rather than just representing it. Her husband drove her from his home in disgust, whereupon Anne Askew moved to London, where she became involved with other Protestants and began distributing leaflets which some claimed to be heretical. She also took to public preaching, earning herself the nickname of 'the fair gospeller'. After a while, Anne's husband decided that this scandalous behaviour was making him a laughing-stock and so he had his wife arrested and brought home. She didn't stay long, but returned to London, where she was arrested for heresy. After being released once, she was arrested for the second time on 19 June 1546.

It was unfortunate for Anne Askew that Henry VIII was at that time trying to make alliances in Europe which made it politic for him to back-pedal on the Reformation, of which he had been such an enthusiastic proponent. Some in his government suspected that his wife, Catherine Parr, was a Protestant and saw an opportunity to implicate her by getting Anne Askew to testify against her. Henry's court was a hotbed of intrigue, with different factions working towards various ends and it was all too easy to fall foul of the wrong people, especially in matters of religion.

After some initial questioning, Anne was taken to the Tower of London, where she was shown the rack and invited to name any other Protestants of whom she knew. She declined to do so and was ordered to remove all her clothes, except her shift. She was then fastened to the rack by her ankles and wrists and two of the king's ministers themselves undertook the torture. One of these men was the Lord Chancellor, Sir Richard Rich, and he actually turned the wheels of the rack with his own hands. Anne fainted, whereupon she was revived and the torture repeated. Her screams could be heard all across the grounds of the Tower and so disturbed was Sir Anthony Kingston, the Constable of the Tower, that he refused to have any further part in the proceedings and left to seek out the king. In the event, Anne Askew revealed nothing at all. The torture had been a waste of time. Her hips, shoulders, elbows and knees had all been pulled from their sockets though and she was crippled and in the utmost agony. A month later, Anne Askew was taken to Smithfield to be burned at the stake with three men who were also Protestants and had been convicted of heresy.

So severe were Anne Askew's injuries, that she was still in great pain four weeks after being racked. Her limbs were quite useless and she had to be carried to the place of execution in a chair. On 16 July,1546, the 26-year-old Anne was brought to Smithfield and offered the chance to save her life if she would renounce her religious beliefs. She replied to this offer by saying firmly, 'I came not thither to deny my Lord and master'. Before they were burned, the four condemned heretics were forced to listen to a sermon preached to them, attempting to convince them of the error of their ways. Despite the pain she was in, Anne Askew listened attentively to what Bishop Shaxton said. When she agreed with what was being expounded, she nodded vigorously to show her approval. At other times though, she shook her head and said loudly, 'There he misseth, and speaketh without the book.' Because she was quite unable to stand, a seat had been fixed to Anne's stake and she was chained to this and the fire lit. It is said that it was not until the flames reached her chest that the pain made her scream.

The Tudor monarchs grew very fond of the rack and this was noticed by ordinary people. Although they were not themselves subject to torture, unless they became involved with plots to overthrow the monarch or were foolish enough to belong to the wrong religious group, there were murmurs of disapproval about the extent to which first Henry VIII and then his daughter Elizabeth resorted so readily to torture.

The rack was not the only instrument of torture being used in England during the sixteenth century. Another, even more ingenious device was installed in the Tower of London, one not seen anywhere else in the world. This was the 'Scavenger's Daughter' or 'Skeffington's Gyves' and it worked in precisely the opposite way to the rack. Instead of stretching the unfortunate subject, he was squeezed and compressed.

Sir Leonard Skeffington (or Skevington) was for a time Lieutenant of the Tower of London during the reign of Henry VIII. He was responsible for introducing the new method of torture to the Tower. Just as the rack became known colloquially as the Duke of Exeter's Daughter, so too was Skeffington's device knowns as 'Skevington's Daughter', of which 'Scavenger's Daughter' is a corruption. Those being tortured in it were said to be 'married to the Scavenger's Daughter'. Illustration 7 shows somebody being crushed in this strange machine. Its shape was rather like a horse's stirrup, except that the two curved parts which rose from the base were not joined together, but rather left open, although joined by a screw. It was used in the following way.

The person being interrogated was made to kneels on the base plate and then lean forward, until his chest was resting on his thighs. The hoops were then closed over his back and screwed shut, harder and harder. Breathing became all but impossible, ribs might crack and sometimes the spine would be damaged. It was not uncommon for blood to be forced from the nose and ears. This particular instrument of torture can be quite hard to visualize and a number of inaccurate and misleading pictures have been published of the Scavenger's Daughter.

Writing in the seventeenth century, Matthew Tanner described the action of Skeffington's Gyves in detail:

> The Scavenger's daughter constricts and binds into a ball. This holds the body in a threefold manner, the lower legs pressed to the thigh, the thighs to the belly, and thus both are locked with two iron cramps which are pressed by the tormentor his force against each other into a circular form; the body of the victim almost broken by this compression. By the cruel torture, more dreadful and more complete than the rack, by the cruelty of which the whole body is bent that with some the blood exudes from the tips of the hands and feet, with others the box of the chest being burst, a quantity of blood is expelled from the mouth and nostrils.

In 1580, two Jesuits were subjected to the embrace of the Scavenger's Daughter. It should be mentioned that during Elizabeth I's reign, Catholics who were tortured and executed suffered not for their religion, but rather because of their treason. Because they did not acknowledge the queen as head of the Church in England, devout and militant Catholics were widely regarded as traitors. This is made clear by the charge against Thomas Coteham and Lucas Kerbie. They were charged that, 'Contrary both to love and duty, they forsook their native country, to live beyond the seas under the Pope's obedience.' After returning to England, the pair were arrested and taken on 5 December 1580 to the Tower of London, where they were both put into Skeffington's Gyves and questioned. It is said that Coteham, 'bled profusely from the nose'. Both were later hanged, drawn and quartered for high treason.

On 10 March 1581, the same year that Thomas Coteham and Lucas Kerbie were executed, an Irishman called Thomas Miagh was accused of treason, by leading a rebellion in Ireland, and brought to the Tower. Miagh refused to admit anything and so after a while, he was tortured. The official report says that:

We subjected him to the torture of Skevington's Iron and with so much sharpness as was in our judgement convenient, yet can we get from him no further matter.

Despite the torture, Miagh refused to confess and he was held prisoner in the Tower for the next two years. There is to this day a memento of him in the Beauchamp Tower of the Tower of London. After his ordeal in the Scavenger's Daughter, he painstakingly carved a graffito on one of the stone walls. It reads:

THOMAS MIAGH – WHICH LETH HERE THAT FAYNE WOLD
FROM HENS BE GON BY TORTURE STRAUNGE MI TROUTH
WAS TRYED YET OF MY LIBERTY DENIED

The 'torture straunge' is of course a reference to the unusual device used to torment him.

If England had always been somewhat ambivalent and reserved about using torture during interrogations, there was a neighbouring country which had no hesitation in resorting to extreme measures when those being questioned showed a reluctance to speak at once. In Scotland, torture was accepted as being both a useful aid to criminal investigation and also an excellent way of deterring crime in the first place by making a frightful example of those who ended up being convicted of various offences.

Chapter 2

Torture in Scotland

Scotland has, historically, always had an entirely different attitude to torture than that seen in England. We have seen that although torture was used in England, it was restricted to political cases and then used sparingly and with many reservations. In Scotland, there were no such inhibitions. Torture was an accepted part of the judicial process and great ingenuity was exercised in inventing brutal ways to inflict pain on those suspected of criminal offences. Torture was not only used regularly in extracting confessions, but it was also used as part of the death penalty in ways which were never seen in any other part of the British Isles. We shall begin our examination of the Scottish approach to torture by looking at one or two examples of particularly savage executions which involved the use of torture.

At the beginning of 1437, Walter Stewart, the Earl of Atholl, decided to assassinate King James I of Scotland and seize power for his own family. As son of King Robert II, he felt that he had some claim to the throne. The Earl of Atholl's grandson was part of this planned coup. A small group of men, including Sir Robert Graham who actually stabbed the king to death, stormed the royal apartments in Perth on 20 February 1437 and the king was killed. There was, however, no popular support for the claims to the throne of the Earl of Atholl and the plan collapsed. Those concerned in the king's death fled. James' wife, Queen Joan, was a strong-minded woman and she managed to rally support for the dead king's son as rightful heir to the throne. Within a few weeks, the plotters were hunted down. Even by medieval standards, the vengeance exacted on those who had assassinated the king was astonishingly savage.

The first two men concerned in the murder of the king to be captured were Robert Stewart and Christopher Chambers. There was to be no trial; judgement had already been given before they were caught. The two of them were taken to Edinburgh, where an especially high scaffold had been constructed. A huge crowd watched as they were stripped naked and bound to wooden crosses. Then the executioner used a pair of red-hot pincers to rip pieces of flesh from their bodies. But this was only the beginning of what they were to endure. They were taken down and paraded through the streets, with the executioner tearing at them with his pincers while they walked through the crowds. The two men were then taken to another scaffold, where they were compelled to stand for two hours, bleeding heavily, as those watching them hurled insults and callous jokes at them. Then they were taken to another part of the city and hoisted up by ropes under their armpits, so that everybody could have another look at them. The show concluded with Robert Stewart being torn apart by four horses which had been harnessed to his arms and legs. Christopher Chambers was merely beheaded.

Incredibly, Christopher Chambers and Robert Stewart got off lightly compared to the Earl of Atholl. The 70-year-old earl was first brought out before the crowds quite naked and hoisted into the air by his ankles on a primitive crane which had been erected. Then he was allowed to fall, but stopped short before hitting the ground. This was repeated several times, until his legs had been jerked out of their sockets. He was then returned to his cell until the next day. As the chief instigator of the conspiracy to murder her husband, the widowed queen intended that Walter Stewart's suffering should not be over quickly.

The Earl of Atholl had encouraged people to join themselves to his enterprise by claiming that he had consulted a seer or witch who had foretold that he would be 'crowned before a multitude'. Shades of *Macbeth*! Queen Joan was happy to aid in the fulfilment of this prophecy. On the day after his legs had been torn from their sockets, the old earl was brought out and tied to a pillar. An iron crown had been made and inscribed with the words, 'King of Traitors'. This was heated in a fire until it was glowing red-hot. It was then placed on the head of the Earl of Atholl. He was taken back to prison. On the third day, he was taken out into public again and stretched out on the scaffold. An incision was then made in his stomach and his intestines pulled out and burned. Finally, his heart was cut out and thrown in a fire and the decapitated head of the traitor placed on a spike, with the iron crown upon it.

It was now time for the climax of these ghastly public tortures. The man who had actually killed King James, by plunging a dagger into his chest, was Sir Robert Graham. He had also been caught, hiding under a rock which is still to this day known as 'Graham's Rock'. He was executed in Stirling. King James' widow wanted the suffering of the regicides to be seen in as many parts of Scotland as possible, which is why the executions took place in different cities. The condemned man was placed naked in a cart in which there was a pole, 7ft high. To this, his right hand was fixed, by hammering through it the dagger with which he had stabbed the king. The cart was then driven through the streets of Stirling. Two men tore at Robert Graham's body with red-hot pliers, tormenting him the whole way. When they reached the execution-ground, his right hand was cut off and burnt. He was then nailed to the pole by his left hand and paraded once more through Stirling.

When he was returned to his cell for the night, somebody threw a blanket over the gravely-injured man, which, although meant as an act of kindness, was to cause him dreadful suffering the next day. In the morning, Graham was taken to be executed. When they arrived at the place where he was to die, the blanket was pulled off. During the night, it had stuck to all his wounds and the pain was so great that he fainted. When he recovered, he said that this had hurt more than the original tortures of the previous day. Robert Graham's son, who had been involved in the planned seizure of the throne, was brought forth and beheaded in front of him. Then he too had his head removed.

This grim account of one of the most terrible series of executions ever to be held in the British Isles suggests that the Scots were very good at coming up with ways of inflicting pain on those whom they felt deserved it. Excruciating pain was used not only for those being punished for crimes of which they had been convicted, but also to wring confessions from suspects. The methods in Scotland were infinitely more varied than those adopted by the less-imaginative English. A case in the Orkney islands at the end of the sixteenth century gives some idea of the range of tortures used north of the border.

In 1594, the Orkney Islands were a Scottish possession, under the control of Patrick Stewart, 2nd Earl of Orkney. He was generally known in the islands as 'Black Patie'. Black Patie was on bad terms with his brothers, whom he suspected, quite rightly, of wishing him dead. One younger brother, acting on behalf of them all, consulted a local healer or witch called Allison Balfour, who allegedly advised him on the proper way to cast a spell to cause the death of his brother. When Black Patie caught wind of this, he had one of his brothers' servants arrested and tortured. This man had poison in his possession. From him, he got the name of Allison Balfour and so had her and her entire family arrested and brought in for questioning. We note here a difference between England and Scotland in the use of torture. In England, only men were tortured to discover information. There is only one case on record of a woman being legally tortured in England during an interrogation; in Scotland though, women were just as likely to be treated in this way as men.

The first step in the process was to screw an iron frame onto Allison Balfour's bare legs. This was called the cashilaws and it could be heated by a furnace so as to burn the bare flesh against which it was pressing. The woman was kept in the cashilaws for two days, with the device being repeatedly heated, until Allison Balfour fainted. Each time she recovered, the torture was resumed. Despite this, no admissions were obtained. A particularly shocking aspect of the affair is that the torture was carried out by a man called Henry Colville, who was a church minister. His involvement is explained by the fact that this was, nominally at least, a witchcraft case. The minister was also a close friend of Black Patie, which is why he took a particularly close interest in the case.

When it was plain that torturing Allison Balfour herself was not going to be effective, Colville turned his attentions to her family. He had her husband brought into his wife's presence and stretched out on the floor. Over 700lbs of stone was piled onto the man's chest, until he was almost at the point of death, but still, the woman said nothing. Then her son was brought in and tortured with the boots.

The boots were used extensively in Europe and they had been adopted in Scotland as a very effective, if hideous, way of torturing suspects and making them confess. Two different types of this torture were used regularly in Scotland. In one, a tube made of four planks of wood bound together with rope was placed around the lower part of the leg, from the knee to the ankle. Other pieces of wood were then squeezed in and wedges were driven between these and the sides of the 'boot', so compressing the leg. This was the type of boot used on Allison Balfour's son. No fewer than fifty-seven blows were given with the hammer, but his mother still refused to admit anything.

Finally, Allison Balfour's seven-year-old daughter was brought in and her fingers secured in a type of vice known in Scotland as the pilliwinkies. This was a primitive device for crushing fingers; in design rather like a pair of nutcrackers. Hearing the little girl's screams was too much and her mother then confessed to all that was suggested. On 16 December 1594, Allison Balfour was strangled and then burned at the stake for witchcraft. Before her execution, she made a public statement, repudiating her confession and detailing the various tortures used against her and her family.

There are two things about this account which immediately strike us as being very different from the way that things were being done at that time in England. In England, there was just one rack and one set of Skeffington's Gyves. These were kept in the capital and used only in cases where there was a suspicion of treason. In Scotland, even a remote province like the Orkneys had its own set of torture devices ready to use for any case which was thought to require urgent investigation. The second thing which strikes us if the indiscriminate use of torture. Allison Balfour's little daughter could have known nothing of any supposed plot against the Earl of Orkney and yet it was considered perfectly proper to use a thumbscrew on her as a way of increasing the pressure on her mother. In England, torture was used sparingly and in special cases; in Scotland, it was available at the drop of the proverbial hat.

Executions which featured torture before death were also more common in Scotland than they were in England. It is true that the prescribed English way of disposing of traitors – hanging, drawing and quartering – was a disgusting spectacle, designed to make death as painful as it could be for the criminal, but this was an established procedure, whose details would have been well-known to anybody contemplating treason. In Scotland, grotesque executions were arranged on an ad hoc basis, if a crime was thought to be worthy of an especially gruesome punishment. We saw this in the case of the Earl of Atholl. Another instance of this tendency was the occasional use of breaking on the wheel, a popular method of torturing people to death which was widely used on the Continent. This meant that the condemned man was tied to a large cartwheel and then had his limbs broken with an iron bar or hammer. The shins were often broken first, followed by the thighs and arms. Depending upon the nature of the crime, the victim could then be killed outright with a blow to the chest or neck. For murders with aggravating features, the mangled person would be left to suffer for some hours or even overnight, only being strangled or having his neck broken when it was decided that he had suffered enough. Illustration 8 is of a man being broken on the wheel, one of the most hideous deaths imaginable.

Breaking on the wheel was never used in England, but there are a number of instances of its taking place in Scotland, in each case as a consequence of some remarkable feature of the murders for which the men were condemned to death, which made their crimes worse than usual. In 1571, for instance, Trooper Cawdor was broken on the wheel for the murder of Matthew Lennox, who was acting as regent for his grandson, James I, who would one day become King of England as well. The murder of the regent was seen as being on a par with treason and so deserving a dreadful death.

On 30 April 1591, another breaking on the wheel took place in Edinburgh. John Dickson was convicted of murdering his own father some years earlier and immediately taken to the cross in the city centre and executed. Parricide, the murder of one's father, was also seen as being similar to treason and so deserving of the most condign punishment. There was one more aspect of this crime which was seen as being abhorrent to the sensitivities of the time. John Dickson had been excommunicated and during this ecclesiastical process, had denied that he had committed the murder. This was perjury of the most blatant and hardened sort and would alone have called for severe retribution. Dickson was tied to a cartwheel and his limbs broken. He was not killed, but left alive to suffer until the next day.

Another crime which was treated as being a form of treason was the murder of a master by a servant, it being thought that servants had an allegiance to their employers similar in some ways to that owned by a subject to a monarch. In England, this kind of crime was called *petit treason* and women were burned at the stake for it, rather than just being hanged. In Scotland, it could end in being broken on the wheel. The wife of the Laird of Warristoune arranged for her husband to be murdered, entering into a conspiracy with the laird's horse-boy and two of her female servants. Robert Weir, who looked after the stable, entered the laird's bedroom and stabbed him to death. The crime was detected though and although Robert Weir escaped, the wife and female servants were arrested, brought to trial, convicted of murder, and then executed. Class distinctions at that time meant that while the wife of the laird was beheaded, her servants were burned at the stake.

It was to be three years before Robert Weir was captured and when he was, the court's sentence on him was a ferocious one; he was to be broken upon the wheel. The execution took place at the cross in Edinburgh. A scaffold was erected and a cartwheel fixed in position. Robert Weir was tied to this and then, using the coulter of a plough, a long iron shaft, the hangman broke the young man's limbs. He began by shattering the shins and then worked his way around the other limbs. It was a lengthy and exquisitely painful death. Afterwards, by order of the court, the mangled body was left on display for twenty-four hours.

When a Scottish king became the king also of England, it was only to be expected that he should expect torture to be a part of the process of questioning in London, just as it had been in Edinburgh. James VI of Scotland, whom we saw in Chapter 1 directing the torture of a suspected witch, was not popular with Catholics. Two years after he became King of England in 1603, a group of Catholics decided to murder James and destroy Parliament, by the use of a huge quantity of gunpowder, an event commemorated to this day in Britain as Guy Fawkes' Night.

Guy Fawkes was caught on the night of 4 November 1605 in the cellars of Parliament, surrounded by thirty-six barrels of gunpowder. There could hardly be a clearer case of a man being caught red-handed! Nevertheless, Fawkes, who was going at that time by the startlingly unoriginal pseudonym of 'John Johnson', refused to talk. He was taken to the king on 5 November, but would not explain the details of the failed plot. It is some indication of how readily King James' mind should turn to torture in such a case, that just twenty-four hours later, on 6 November, he should issue an order for Guy Fawkes to be tortured. The king himself wrote down a list of the questions which should be put to Guy Fawkes when he was being tortured, such as 'If he was a Papist, who brought him up in it?'

As we saw in Chapter 1, torture could only be applied on direct orders from either the Privy Council or the monarch. In this case, the king himself not only gave the specific questions which were to be asked, he also described how the process of interrogation should proceed. He wrote, 'the gentler Tortures are to be first used unto him *et sic per gradus ad ima tenditur*', or, in English, 'and so by degrees proceeding to the worst'. By the next day, this had proved most effective and Guy Fawkes had given all the information required of him.

In the next chapter, we shall see how torture was declared unlawful in England, just twenty-five years after the capture of those involved in the Gunpowder Plot, but since the kings of England were also now the kings too of Scotland, there was no reason why torture should stop there. Throughout the seventeenth century, torture of suspects not only continued in Scotland, it went from strength to strength, with new methods being introduced.

Readers might have been more than a little surprised to read of King James referring to 'the gentler Tortures'. Can there be such a thing as a 'gentle' torture?

The same expression was used in Scotland a few years later during an investigation into a supposed case of witchcraft. In 1618, Margaret Barclay, who lived in Ayrshire, was accused of sinking a ship by witchcraft. A tramp called John Stewart was charged with having precognition of the event, that is to say, he had used magic to foretell the future. In terror of being tortured, Stewart implicated a woman called Isobel Insh, who was also taken into custody. She attempted to escape, by climbing out of a window and onto the roof of a church, but slipped and fell to her death.

Meanwhile, John Stewart could not face the prospect of being tortured and so managed to strangle himself, leaving Margaret Barclay alone to face the music. Because she persisted in denying that she was a witch, the Earl of Eglinton, who was taking a hand in the case, decided that she should be tortured. To reassure those who had reservations about the torture of a woman though, the earl declared that the means used would be what he described as, 'a most safe and gentle torture'. This meant placing the woman's bare legs in the stocks and, 'thereafter by on-laying of certain iron bars'. The dreadful pain of having iron bars piled up on one's shins can only be imagined and it is little surprise that after enough had been laid on her legs and the weight slowly increased, that Margaret Barclay eventually cried, 'Take off! Take off! And before God I shall show you the whole form.' It is one thing, however, to force a confession from somebody under torture, it is quite another matter to get them to confirm what they have said later in court. When she was tried for witchcraft, Margaret Barclay said to the court, 'All I have confessed was in agony of torture, and before God all I have spoken is false and untrue.' Nevertheless, she was strangled and her body burned at the stake.

While enduring the extreme pain of this 'safe and gentle torture', Margaret Barclay had named another woman as a witch, one Isobel Crawford. She too was taken and questioned in the same way. According to a contemporary report, the wretched woman endured the ordeal of having her shins loaded with iron and;

> admirably, without any kind of din or exclamation, suffer above 30 stone
> of iron to be laid on her legs, never shrinking thereat in any sort, but
> remaining, as it were, steady.

In the end though, Isobel Crawford, like Margaret Barclay, could stand no more and agreed to say what was required of her. She too recanted of her confession in court, but was found guilty and executed.

Readers who are wondering what King James might have had in mind when he recommended that Guy Fawkes first have the 'gentler tortures' used on him, will no doubt recollect that hanging by the manacled wrists was thought to be a fairly mild way of persuading men to speak. When a man is implicated though in attempting to kill not only the king, but also all the lords and Members of

Parliament in the country, then it is not surprising that the 'gentler tortures, were dispensed with after a very short time. That the obdurate Guy Fawkes spilled the beans after only twenty-four hours suggests strongly that something a little firmer than just leaving him in an uncomfortable position for the night was resorted to!

Knowing that torture was not prohibited by Scottish law, in the way that it was acknowledged to be in England from 1628 onwards, a development at which we shall be looking in the next chapter, came in quite handy for the English monarchs of the seventeenth century. Since they were all, from James I onwards, kings and queens of Scotland as well as England, there was no reason why a prisoner held in London, where torture was forbidden, should not be transported to Edinburgh, where it was not. This procedure, something like the modern practice of so-called 'extraordinary rendition' was used during times of unrest, such as the years between 1670 and the Glorious Revolution of 1688. The Scots were keeping up to date with new and improved methods of torture and some of these innovative techniques were yielding faster results, with much less visible damage to the bodies of those being interrogated than the rack or Scavenger's Daughter.

A renowned Scottish Royalist was held in the Tower of London after the end of the English Civil War. In 1652, he escaped and fled, first to Europe and then on to Moscow. Thomas Dalyell was so famous as a military man, that he was eventually made a general in the Russian army, acquiring on his return home to Britain the nickname 'The Muscovy General'. When Thomas Dalyell came back to his own country, on the restoration of the monarchy in 1660, he brought with him an ingenious invention which had caught his eye while he was soldiering in Russia. Crushing fingers had been a common way of getting people to talk in Scotland since at least the early fifteenth century. This had been done by squeezing fingers and thumbs with the pilliwinkies, which worked like nutcrackers. What General Dalyell saw in operation in Russia, though, were real thumbscrews, designed to crush both thumbs at once and with a wingnut that could be tightened both to increase and also maintain indefinitely the pressure. These became a standard tool in the rooting out of traitors and malcontents. Thumbscrews proved so useful in persuading reluctant people to confess, that they remained in use as late as the Second World War. They were a favourite of the Gestapo and Illustration 9 shows one of these ingenious devices. Using the thumbscrews required no special training and they could be made by any competent blacksmith.

In the late 1670s and early 1680s, there was a fear that Charles II might become Catholic, as was his brother, soon to be King James II. There was a lot of disquiet about this, not least in Scotland with its tradition of Calvinism. The best way to uncover any plots was thought to be to torture those who might be expected to have any knowledge of such things and so learn from them the names of others who might be planning mischief. In 1668, a preacher called James Mitchell tried to assassinate the Archbishop of St Andrews. He fired at the prelate, but missed, wounding a bystander in the wrist. It was to be almost ten years before James Mitchell was brought to justice, but when he was, the authorities were very keen to find out who he had been with and if there were any other plans for violence against the Established Church in Scotland.

James Mitchell was brought before the Privy Council on 18, 22, and 24 January 1676 and tortured with the boot. This was the wooden boot, described above. When the Privy Council found that Mitchell refused to answer their questions, they sent for the executioner, who brought with him the tools necessary for the job. James Mitchell was tied to a chair and his left leg placed in the 'boot'. He took it out and placed his right leg in it instead, saying, 'Take the best of the two, for I freely bestow it in the cause.' Then the serious questioning began. The Council asked a great deal about where Mitchell had been and what he had been doing. He answered vaguely, larding his answers with long quotations from Scripture. When it was plain that they would not get any information from him, the executioner was given the go-ahead to begin his work. After placing wooden staves in the boot, the executioner pushed in a wooden wedge and then began hammering this in with a mallet. Again, the questions were asked, but at the ninth blow of the mallet, the victim fainted from the pain. The executioner cried, 'Alas my lords, he is gone!' Once Mitchell had been revived, the torture was continued, but all to no avail. James Mitchell was subsequently convicted of attempted murder and hanged.

General Dalyell, the man who brought back the thumbscrews from Russia, was a keen and enthusiastic exponent of the use of torture, having, it is supposed, picked up a good working knowledge of the practice while he was in the Russian army. After he returned to Scotland, he was very keen to see men tortured and behaved as though he were something of an authority on the subject. We have looked in detail at one form of the Scottish 'boot', but there was a second and even more painful form, which was the metal 'boot'. This was no more than a large metal boot, which rose to the height of the knee. It was placed on the foot of the person to be questioned and then wooden or metal wedges were put in it, between the metal sides of the boot and the flesh of the victim. These were then hammered in, lacerating the flesh and sometimes breaking the bones. There was scope for increasing the pain of this torture, for instance by hammering the wedges against the shins, rather than the fleshy calves.

During the seventeenth century, torture in Scotland became a little more regulated than had previously been the case. In the sixteenth century, any local magistrate might undertake to put a suspect to the boot, but now it could only be done in the presence of the Privy Council. Because these were the men who authorized the practice, it was thought only right that they actually witnessed what was done in their name and so it became the custom that all members of the council were obliged to be present when torture was taking place. Not all could stand it and there are stories of members of the Privy Council leaving the room in disgust. Giulbert Burnet, who was appointed Bishop of Salisbury under William III, wrote detailed accounts of the torture used in Scotland before the Glorious revolution of 1688. In a book called *History of My Own Time*, he had this to say of the Privy Council's being obliged to watch the torture which they ordered, 'when any are to be struck in the boot, it is done in the presence of the Council, and upon that occasion almost all offer to run away'.

In 1681, a man called John Spreul was arrested, because it was believed that he was involved in a plan to blow up Charles II's brother. Spreul denied everything and so the Privy Council ordered that he should be put to the torture of the boot. The boot used in this instance was the metal one. Bishop Burnet takes up the story:

> The hangman put his foot into the instrument called the boot, and, at every query put to him, gave five strokes or thereby upon the wedges. When nothing could be expiscated in this way, they ordered the old boot to be brought, alleging this new one used by the hangman was not so good as the old, and accordingly it was brought, and he underwent the torture a second time, and adhered to what he had before said. General Dalziel complained at the second torture, that the hangman did not strike hard enough upon the wedges; he said, he struck with all his strength, and offered the general the mall to do it himself.

In the years before the death of Charles II, secret meetings were held with the strongly Protestant William of Orange, who was married to the king's niece Mary. The suspicion was that this was a plot to ensure that James, who was at that time the Duke of York, would not accede to the throne when his brother Charles died. In 1683, a scheme was hatched to assassinate both the king and his brother on their way back from the races at Newmarket. This became known as the Rye House Plot, after the name of the manor house where the ambush of the royal party was to take place. Many arrests followed the discovery of the plan. One of those taken into custody was a Scottish minister called William Carstares, who had been travelling to and from the Netherlands to visit Prince William of Orange. Carstares was arrested in Kent, taken to London and then sent to Edinburgh, where he could legally be tortured, something which had been ruled unlawful in England in 1628.

There are several gruelling accounts of the torture of William Carstares, which was undertaken with a pair of the thumbscrews based on the design of those which General Dalyell had brought back from Moscow. The members of the Privy Council were obliged by law to be present when torture was taking place.

The council called for one of the bailies of Edinburgh, and the executioner with the engine of torture being present, the Lord Chancellor commanded the bailie to cause the executioner to put him in torture by applying the thumbscrews on him, which being done, and he having for the space of an hour continued in the agony of torture the screw being space and space stretched until he appeared near to faint; and they drew him so hard as they put him to extreme torture, so that they could not unscrew them, till the smith who had made them was brought with his tools to take them off.

Here is another account of this session, which was so harrowing that some members of the Privy Council were unable to remain in the room to witness it:

Mr Carstares maintained such a command of himself, that, while the sweat streamed over his brow, and down his cheeks, with the agony he endured, he never betrayed the smallest inclination to depart from his first resolutions. The Earl of Queensbury was so affected, that, after telling the Chancellor that he saw the poor man would rather die than confess, he stepped out of the council, along with the Duke of Hamilton, into another room, both of them being unable longer to witness the scene.

Despite the appalling agony, Carstares refused to admit any part in the plots about which he was questioned and after spending some time in prison, he was released.

There was a curious sequel to William Carstares' session with the thumbscrews. After James II had become king and then been deposed by his own daughter, Mary, and her husband William of Orange, the thumbscrews used on Carstares somehow came into his possession., He enjoyed a glittering career after the flight of James II in 1688, and in some later portraits Carstares is shown holding this gruesome souvenir. When William and Mary became joint rulers of England and Scotland, Carstares was appointed royal chaplain, as a reward for all that he had endured. King William asked to be shown the thumbscrews and when Carstares fetched them, the king expressed a desire to try them out and see if the pain was really as bad as people said. After the royal thumbs had been inserted in the device, the chaplain gave a single turn, being unwilling to hurt the king. William was dissatisfied and told Carstares to turn them more; which was done. 'Harder yet!' said the king, whereupon Carstares gave quite a vigorous twist to the screw, causing the king to cry out in protest. 'Stop, doctor, stop! Another turn would make me confess anything.'

It may be supposed that when William himself felt under threat from conspiracies against him, he must surely have remembered how effective those thumbscrews were, because he was quite willing to use them against anybody suspected of opposing his interests. In 1690, a man called Henry Neville Payne was thought to be part of a plan to restore James II. After his arrest, he was brought to Edinburgh and imprisoned in the castle. King William sent explicit instructions about the treatment to which Payne should be subjected. He wrote that:

> We do require you to examine Nevil Pain strictly; and in case he prove obstinate or disingenuous do you proceed against him to torture, with all the rigour that the law allows in such cases; and not doubting your ready and vigorous applications for the further discovery of what so much concerns the public safety, we bid you farewell.

Neville Payne underwent two sessions of torture, with the boot and the thumbscrews being used on both occasions. Nothing could be got from him, though, and some members of the Privy Council who were, as required, present during the questioning, began to have their doubts about his guilt. One of those present, Lord Crawford, said later that Payne was questioned:

> with all the severity which was consistent with humanity, even unto that pitch that we could not preserve life and have gone further, but without the least success. He was so manly and resolute under his sufferings that such of the Council as were not acquainted with the evidence, were brangled, and began to give him charity that he might be innocent.

At last, since no damaging admissions were forthcoming, Neville Payne was returned to his cell. Despite not being brought to trial, he remained in prison for the next eleven years.

The torture of Neville Payne in 1690 was already something of an anachronism and it was fairly obvious to most people that the trick of sending prisoners north, across the border, so that they could be treated in ways forbidden by the judges of England, was not really on. Since James I came to the throne in 1603, the English and Scottish crowns had been combined, so that although England and Scotland remained separate countries, they had the same monarch. In 1707, the Parliaments too combined and from that year onwards, both countries became united as Great Britain. In both England and Scotland, from that time use of torture in questioning prisoners was absolutely forbidden.

Chapter 3

The Decline of Torture in
Seventeenth-Century England

It might have been thought that with the exposure of the Gunpowder Plot, accomplished only with the use of torture on the principle conspirator, that the wind was set fair for the future of torture in England and that it would continue to be a most useful tool for the state, just as it had been throughout the Tudor era. This must have looked particularly likely, since a Scottish king now sat on the throne of England, a man who had grown up in a country where torture was considered an indispensable part of the judicial process. As we saw in the last chapter, the ambivalent attitude towards the use of torture as an aid to interrogation, which was so common in England, was unknown in Scotland. There, torture to obtain information and force confessions was merely a given fact of life. Yet within a few years, the rack was to be consigned to history and torture as an adjunct to the questioning of suspects, even in cases of treason, was to be declared illegal in England. There were several milestones which led to this, one man having a very great influence which has lasted to this day.

Sir Edward Coke was Attorney General at the time of the Gunpowder Plot and knew therefore that a warrant had been signed by the king, authorizing the torture of Guy Fawkes. His conscience did not seem to trouble him about the matter at that time; at any rate, he was able to prosecute the plotters, making use of the evidence obtained by torture. It was only in his later years that he began to have reservations about torture and agonised over its lawfulness. What finally caused the greatest lawyer of the age to come down firmly against torture was that the practice depended ultimately on the sovereign being above and beyond the law of the land. Once he was no longer Attorney General, Edward Coke realized that the monarch must be subject to the law, just like everybody else. He or she could not, merely by signing a warrant, act and cause others to act in a way which was not specifically permitted under the law.

The declaring of torture to be illegal must be seen in the context of the struggle in early seventeenth century England to limit and define the power of the sovereign, a process which ultimately resulted in the English Civil War. Men like Edward Coke were beginning to see that the absolutist views of the monarchy held by kings like James I were inimical to the rights of the average subject. If, by signing a warrant, the king could order a supposedly innocent man to be racked, then the rule of law was cast into hazard. Both King James and his son, Charles I realized that debates on the legitimacy of torture were, at least in part, coded attacks on the legitimacy of the Crown to do as it pleased.

It has to be said that Coke came very late to this belief, but that once he had decided that this was how matters stood legally, he threw his efforts into persuading everybody else that his ideas on the subject were the correct ones. There is among many people today a vague idea that Magna Carta forbids torture and this is one of the claims which Edward Coke made. Magna Carta had been around for 400 years before Coke expounded this theory and it must be said that neither he nor anybody else had noticed before that Magna Carta had anything at all to say on the subject. Here is the passage which Coke interpreted as being a specific and binding prohibition on the use of torture on suspected criminals. It is Clause 39:

> No free man shall be taken or imprisoned or disseised or outlawed or in any way ruined, nor will we go or send against him, except by the lawful judgement of his peers or by the law of the land.

Reading this through, it is difficult to see how it could be said to ban the use of torture. Coke realized or claimed to realize, once he was no more an agent of the government, that the words, 'in any way ruined' refer to the act of torture. In his magnum opus, *The Second Part of the Institutes of the Laws of England; Concerning the Magna Carta*, published in 1642, Coke set out the view mentioned above, that Magna Carta expressly forbade torture as a mean of interrogation. In the third part of the *Institutes*, published a couple of years later, he went on to say that, 'there is no law to warrant tortures in this land'. This view of Coke's, founded as it was in Magna Carta, has endured for almost 500 years.

These abstruse legal speculations about the precise meaning of a medieval document drawn up to check a previous king's power in the thirteenth century had a very real and practical effect upon the power of the monarchy under the Stuarts. We can see this in one of the key decisions about the torturing of suspects, taken in what became known as Felton's Case in 1628.

George Villiers, 1st Duke of Buckingham, was a great favourite of James I. Indeed, so affectionate were relations between the two men, that there were strong and persistent rumours that they were actually lovers. Under James' son, Charles I, the Duke of Buckingham continued to be enormously influential, acting as de facto Foreign Secretary and commanding the armed forces in several adventures. When Parliament grew uneasy about Buckingham's power, the king simply dissolved it. It was high-handed actions of this kind which of course led to the civil war which tore the country apart in the 1640s.

Pamphlets were published calling for the assassination of the Duke of Buckingham which, since he was a royal favourite, seemed to smack of an attack on the king himself. It was certainly no particular surprise when, on 23 August 1628, a disgruntled army officer called John Felton stabbed the duke to death. There was no doubt at all about the identity of the murderer, who freely admitted what he had done. The only question was whether he had acted alone or was part of a wider conspiracy. The obvious thing to do was put him on the rack and see what he might say. King Charles, stubborn though he was, knew that this raised the question of the extent to which the king was above the law and could override it when reasons of state so required. While the Privy Council were discussing the question of whether or not Felton should be racked, Charles asked them to rule on whether or not torture was allowed under English law.

Why did an avowed absolutist monarch like Charles I ask what the Privy Council thought, before ordering the torture of a man whom he regarded as being the agent of a treasonable plot? The answer is that John Felton had become something of a public hero for striking down the Duke of Buckingham. The king thought it unwise to put such a popular figure to torture and hoped to obtain the approval of others for this step, so that the responsibility would not rest with him alone. He could hardly have been pleased with the decision reached!

The Lord Chief Justice was present and King Charles asked him to consult with all his fellow judges and see what their opinion might be. If the law allowed it, said the king, then he would not have to use his prerogative. We look to an account made a few years later to see what the outcome of the judges' deliberations was;

> And having put the question to the Lord Chief Justice, the King commanded him to demand of the resolution of all the judges. And on the 14th November, all the judges being assembled in Sergeants' Inn, in Fleet Street, agreed in one, that he ought not to be tortured because no such punishment is known or allowed by our law.

And that, as far as the torturing of suspects was concerned, was that. Torture was agreed to be an act outside the law and that was the end of the matter.

There was a good deal of hypocrisy about this noble sounding declaration, because one form of dreadful and agonising torture of unconvicted men was to continue for over a hundred years after this decision. The *Peine Forte et Dure* was being used on theoretically innocent men who had not been convicted of any offence until well into the eighteenth century.

There was for many centuries a legal problem with those who refused to plead to an indictment. In other words, when asked to plead guilty or not guilty, there were those who said nothing. Under such circumstances, the law dictated that no trial could take place. From 1345 onwards, it became the custom to commit such stubborn men, and the occasional woman, to close confinement. *Peine Forte et Dure* is a Norman French phrase which means literally, 'hard and strong prison'. Those who were 'mute of malice', to use the official term, and would not plead at their trial, were locked up and given very little food and water until they changed their mind. This could be an annoyingly slow process and so from 1405, things were speeded up a little. From about that time, *Peine Forte et Dure* began to entail being stretched out on one's back and having weights piled upon the chest until the pain became unendurable. Sometimes, this meant that the prisoner was given the chance to plead again in court, but at times, pressing to death was actually the sentence imposed and even if the suspect had a change of heart and agreed to plead one way or the other, weights continued to be heaped on until death resulted. The sentence announced in these cases was chilling:

> That the prisoner should be sent to the prison from whence he came, and put into a mean room, stopped from the light, and shall there be laid on the bare ground, without any litter, straw or other covering, or without any garment about him, except something to hide his privy members. He shall lie upon his back; his head shall be covered and his feet shall be bare. One of his arms shall be drawn with a cord to one side of the room, and the other arm to the other side, and his legs shall be served in the like manner. Then shall there be laid upon his body as much iron or stone as he can bear, and more. The next day he is to have three morsels of barley bread, without drink; and the third day shall have to drink some of the kennel water with bread. And this method is in strictness to be observed until he is dead.

If we take the two forms of judicial torture to be that intended as punishment on the one hand, and on the other, pain, or the threat of pain, inflicted to force the person to say or do something, then it is clear the *Peine Forte et Dure* fell into the second of these categories. Obviously, you do not bother feeding a person who is simply being killed. The diet of bread and water was intended to prolong life, and agony, until the suspected man decided to speak. In short, despite the ruling of the judges in the Felton Case that torture was not permitted in English law, this form of torture would continue.

As the use the *Peine Forte et Dure* became widespread, it was increasingly used not just to extort an answer from a recalcitrant prisoner, but actually as a mode of execution. The bread and water part of the sentence was omitted and the aim was, in many cases reduced to simply crushing the man to death as expeditiously as possible. In Illustration 10, the *Peine Forte et Dure* can be seen being administered in a prison.

The mechanics of this form of torture are best illustrated by looking at an instance which took place during the reign of Elizabeth I. It was, incidentally, the only recorded case of the *Peine Forte et Dure* ever being used on a woman. Before looking at the case of Margaret Clitherow though, we might pause for a moment and ask ourselves why anybody would put themselves through such an ordeal. Surely, if one simply pleaded, then there was a chance of being acquitted and walking free? This was inviting the court to order one to be tortured to death in the most agonising way. The reason was simple and eminently practical. The property of those found guilty of certain crimes – treason was one – was forfeit to the Crown. In short, not only would a family lose the head of the house, they might simultaneously be made homeless and poor. If the person died under the *Peine Forte et Dure*, then he was, technically at least, innocent and his wife and children would be able to retain all his property.

Margaret Clitherow was an ardent and devout Catholic who sheltered priests at her home in York's Shambles, a main street of the old city. This was during the reign of Elizabeth I, when such actions fell within the definition of treason, the Catholic Church denying the queen's right to be head of the Anglican Church. In 1586, Margaret Clitherow was arrested and brought before the York Assizes, charged with harbouring priests. When asked how she pleaded to this charge, she refused to answer. In this case, her intention was to protect her children and servants, all of whom could have been called as witnesses at her trial. She was afraid that if her children refused to give evidence that they might be tortured. The best solution, since she was guilty of the charge, was to die without any trial.

On 25 March 1586, which happened coincidentally to be Good Friday, Margaret Clitherow was stretched out on the floor of a cell. As an act of mercy, to hasten her death, a sharp rock about the size of a man's fist was placed beneath her. When the pressure was great enough, this would break through the ribs and pierce the heart, at least ensuring that death would be mercifully swift. The two sergeants who should have carried out the execution could not bring themselves to kill a woman in this way and so paid four beggars to do it instead. When the preparations were complete, a door was placed on her and piled with 800lbs of stone and iron. She died within fifteen minutes. The house where Margaret Clitherow lived in the Shambles is still standing and nearby is a convent, which houses a most gruesome relic of this episode. After her death, the authorities had Margaret Clitherow's body thrown on a rubbish dump. A Catholic sympathiser cut off one of her hands as a memento to this brave woman. The hand now sits beneath a bell jar in the convent. In 1970, she was canonised and is consequently now a saint of the Catholic Church.

The use of the *Peine Forte et Dure* was widespread in Britain for the whole of the seventeenth and much of the eighteenth centuries. Sometimes, the sharp stone under the back which shortened the suffering was allowed, at other times, not. In 1672, for example, a man called Henry Jones underwent pressing to death but despite being loaded with a mass of iron, he lasted an incredible forty-eight hours. Some were luckier and had the assistance of friends. In 1676 a Major Strangeways killed a lawyer called Fussall who had seduced his sister. He refused to plead when arraigned on a charge of murder, fearing that his estate would be seized by the Crown if he were to be convicted. He obtained permission for some of his friends to be present when he was due to suffer. When the huge quantity of iron piled onto a door laid on Major Strangeways failed to kill him, he begged his friends to help end his agony. They added to the weight by climbing onto the pile of iron, whereupon the major's ribs collapsed and he died at once.

Even when the law insisted on carrying out the *Peine Forte et Dure* until the victim was dead, in practice, if the accused person changed his mind and chose to plead, then he was allowed to do so. In 1723 two highwaymen refused to plead when they were captured and brought to trial. Thirty-three-year-old Thomas Philips and 27-year-old William Spigot were both sentenced to be pressed to death. Philips changed his mind on being taken to the room at Newgate prison where this torture was undertaken. Although he could legally have been subjected anyway to the *Peine Forte et Dure,* he was taken back to court, where he pleaded not guilty. His fellow highwayman was made of sterner stuff and after being stripped, stretched out and having 350lbs piled on his chest, he still refused to plead. When another 50lbs was being added to the weight, he had an abrupt change of heart and agreed to plead. Both men were found guilty and hanged.

In Ireland, the law was applied a little more strictly, as may be seen from a case which took place at Kilkenny in 1740. Matthew Ryan appeared at the assizes, accused of highway robbery. He had not spoken a single word since his arrest and gave the outward impression of being both deaf and dumb. The judges suspected that this was a sham and were most reluctant to see man crushed to death without standing trial. A contemporary writer tells the story of what happened next:

> The judges on this desired the prisoner to plead, but he still pretended to be insensible to all that was said to him. The law called for the *Peine Forte et Dure,* but the judges compassionately deferred awarding it until a future day, in the hope that he might in the meantime acquire a juster sense of his situation. When again brought up, however, the criminal persisted in his refusal to plead: and the court at last pronounced the dreadful sentence, that he should be pressed to death. The sentence was accordingly executed upon him two days after in the public market-place of Kilkenny. As the weights were heaping on the wretched man, he earnestly supplicated to be hanged; but it was beyond the power of

the sheriff to deviate from the mode of punishment prescribed in the sentence, even this was an indulgence which could no longer be granted to him.

Of course, the opposite case occurred from time to time and this was even more tragic. In 1735, a man was pressed to death in Nottingham after having been adjudged 'mute of malice'. It was subsequently discovered that he had been dumb from birth and quite unable to speak even the words 'guilty' or 'not guilty'.

The last known case of the use of the *Peine Forte et Dure* was less than a year after the death of Matthew Ryan. From 1741, the practice fell into disuse and was abolished in 1772. From that time on, when anybody refused to answer a charge, then a plea of 'guilty' was entered. This was changed in 1827 to the present arrangement, whereby anybody who will not enter a plea is assumed to be pleading 'not guilty'.

Despite the ruling of the judges during the Felton Case, torture made a sudden and very localized resurgence during the English Civil War. The circumstances were unusual; in some places during those years, law and order broke down almost entirely. One man saw an opportunity to use torture for his own ends during a time of such chaos, while representing himself as an upright and God-fearing man. It is time to make the acquaintance of Matthew Hopkins, self-styled 'Witchfinder General'.

Until the beginning of the seventeenth century, England traditionally had a more relaxed attitude to witches than the rest of Europe. There were no witch hunts in England during the Tudor period of the kind seen in Germany. Witchcraft was certainly against the law, but the penalties were relatively mild. For instance, under the 1563 Witchcraft Act, harming people or property by casting spells was punishable only by a year's imprisonment. It is true that things changed a little in later years, but there was none of the mass hysteria about the matter that was seen in many European countries at that time. Although some supposed witches were hanged in England during the seventeenth century, there was, except in the case of East Anglia at the time of the English Civil War, no widespread persecution of harmless old women.

Things were very different in Scotland, as we saw in Chapter 2, and when the Scottish king James came to the throne in England, he wanted the English law on witchcraft to be brought into line with that on the Continent and in his own country. The 1604 Witchcraft Statute, passed by the English Parliament, made all acts of witchcraft, from foretelling the future to casting spells, capital crimes on the first offence. From that time onwards, alleged witches were in the same perilous position as they were in mainland Europe and Scotland.

In 1640 or 1641, a young man in his early twenties moved from Suffolk to the Essex town of Manningtree. His father was a Puritan church minister and his son was also very devout, with something of an unhealthy interest in witchcraft. How he made his living is not known, perhaps as a lawyer or legal adviser, but in 1644, two years after the beginning of the English Civil War, this man, Matthew Hopkins, overheard a group of women in Manningtree discussing their dealings with the devil. Things happen in times of war that would not be tolerated in peacetime and sometimes strange hysterias get a grip on ordinary people, ideas that would not be entertained in normal times. So it was, that as the war raged, those living in the strongly Puritan part of the country known as East Anglia began to believe that large numbers of witches were at work, women who lived and among them but owed their allegiance not to God, but rather to the devil. It was an alarming idea, but also a business opportunity.

However Matthew Hopkins had been making his living before, he now saw that his true vocation was to oppose the activities of the devil in Essex and the surrounding counties and to launch a counter-attack on behalf of the Lord. A travelling witchfinder called John Stearne passed through Manningtree and recognized in Hopkins a talented man who could be useful to him. Stearne was in his thirties, about ten years older than Matthew Hopkins, and the pair of them set off to Chelmsford, the county town of Essex. There, they soon uncovered a large coven of witches operating and as a result of their investigations, twenty-nine women were arrested, of whom fifteen were hanged.

Hopkins and Stearne hired themselves out to towns on a no win, no fee basis. In other words, they only required payment if they were able to obtain confessions from the suspected witches which would stand up in court. Once the executions had taken place, they would get the money. In addition to these fees, they expected to be provided with board and lodging in the villages and towns where they stayed. Since there was a genuine fear that the devil was at work in the eastern counties of England, this seemed like a good deal for some town councils. It was in getting the women, and occasional man, to confess to having formed pacts with the devil that Matthew Hopkins and John Stearne had to resort to torture.

In the usual way of things of course, torturing suspects would have been recognized immediately as an illegal act, but the circumstances in which these two 'witchfinders' operated were not at all usual. For one thing, law and order were on the verge of breaking down in some parts of England, as Parliament and the king fought for control. This had led to cases of lynching of women suspected to be in league with the devil. It was thought better that investigations into witchcraft were at least conducted by the authorities, rather than having mobs taking justice into their own hands. This was one reason that those in charge of towns in East Anglia were prepared to cooperate with Matthew Hopkins; the alternative might be chaos and mob rule.

A blind eye was turned to torture in this instance for what seemed like another good reason. Devil worship and causing harm by magic were both viewed by the law as being in a class of their own. On the Continent, such crimes were described as *crimen exceptum*, the very fact of the accusation invalidated the innocence of the accused person. In other words, there was a presumption of guilt. James I's Witchcraft Act had brought this idea into English law and so the women suspected of witchcraft were assumed to be guilty and any means of persuading them to admit their guilt were thought to be acceptable.

Of course, Hopkins and Stearne did not have a rack to use and nor did they have thumbscrews or other such useful devices. Nevertheless, they managed well enough with a little ingenuity. Indeed, so effective were their methods that they even succeeded in persuading an Anglican clergyman to confess to being a wizard! Their methods were crude, but most effective.

In addition to tracking down and extorting confessions from those whom they genuinely believed to be witches, Matthew Hopkins and his assistants were always ready to curry favour with communities by helping rid them of unpopular people that they would like to see the back of. By 1645, Hopkins had eclipsed his mentor, John Stearne, and was in business on his own account, employing a team of helpers who did the actual work of torturing those who would not confess freely. In the Suffolk village of Brandeston, Hopkins heard of an old clergyman whose parishioners disliked him heartily and wished to see removed from his post. As a Justice of the Peace in the nearby town of Framlingham put it, John Lowes was, 'a contentious man and made his parishioners very uneasy, and they were glad to take the opportunity of those wicked times and get him hanged, rather than not get rid of him'. It was the work of a moment to accuse him of being a wizard and Hopkins' men then set out to secure his confession. It looked, on the face of it, a tough job. Here was a very dedicated man of God, 80 years of age and whose entire life had been spent in the service of the church. Surely, he would be unlikely to admit to witchcraft?

The Reverend John Lowes lasted just three days, before breaking down and admitting that he had made a pact with the devil and cast a spell which caused a ship to sink with the loss of all on board her, off the Essex coast at Harwich. He further confessed that he was visited daily by six imps, who helped him create mischief in the neighbourhood. All that had been necessary to make the old vicar confess was that the men working for Matthew Hopkins had

> kept him awake for several nights together, and ran him backwards and forwards about the room until he was out of breath. Then they rested

him a little and then ran him again. And thus they did for several days and nights together, till he was weary of his life and was scarce sensible of what he said and did.

Easy when you know how! We recall what some ancient writers had to say on the subject of torture, that it is best avoided because it is as likely to bring forth falsehood as it is truth.

After confessing, the Rev. Lowes was taken to Framlingham Castle, tied up and thrown in the moat. He floated, which was of course the final and infallible sign that he had rejected God. The 'swimming' of witches was of course nothing more than the ordeal of cold water, which we saw being used in Chapter 1. Although the use of this ordeal had fallen into disuse since it was frowned upon by the Catholic Church in the thirteenth century, it had come back in vogue in England, since James I became king. When he was king only of Scotland, James had written a book on witchcraft with the intriguing title, *Demonology*. In it, he gave his approval to the use of the cold water ordeal in cases of suspected witchcraft, by stating that:

So it appears that God hath appointed, for a supernatural sign of the monstrous impiety of witches, that the water shall refuse to receive them in her bosom, that have shaken off them the sacred water of baptism and wilfully refused benefit thereof.

This, then, was the clincher. Having obtained a detailed confession relating to such things as dealings with imps and wrecking ships by means of the black arts, the fact that John Lowes floated on the moat, rather than sinking, was proof positive of his wicked nature. He was taken to Bury St Edmunds, where other witches were on trial and there convicted of being a warlock. On 27 August 1645, he was hanged.

There was uneasiness, though, about the revival of the ordeal by cold water. Tying a person's right thumb to their left big toe and chucking them in the nearest river or pond might have been a simple and effective way of demonstrating guilt, but a Parliamentary commission ordered Matthew Hopkins to abandon the practice. Not everybody was convinced that East Anglia was suffering a sudden infestation of witches and wizards and eyebrows were being raised at the number of harmless old people who were being hanged.

Even without 'swimming' suspects, Hopkins and his men had a number of tricks at their disposal. The man now styling himself 'Witchfinder General' had discovered that witches were only able to summon up their familiar spirits, imps and demons who did their bidding, when they were relaxed and cheerful. Obviously then, the thing to do was make sure that those arrested were anything but. This was achieved by 'watching', which in plain language meant sleep deprivation.

The suspects were watched and woken up if they showed any signs of dozing off. They were also 'run', as John Lowes had been, until they were exhausted. A few days of this treatment was usually enough to break most of the women accused of witchcraft. It must be remembered that they were mostly old and less able to withstand being deprived of sleep and made to undergo physical exertion than a younger person would be.

Deliberate humiliation was also inflicted upon the supposed witches. Hopkins claimed that witches often had a secret nipple, from which they fed their familiars. In the case of John Lowes, he had found this on the top of the man's head. The women were stripped naked and every inch of their body was examined for any unusual marks. These could be moles, warts, tags of skin, pretty well anything out of the ordinary. They could be identified as a mark of the devil, because they were insensitive to pain. Bodkins and pins were pressed into these imperfections and the absence of a cry of pain was taken as evidence that the mark was supernatural. Of course, by the time the women had been tormented for days, exhausted, stripped and made to run around a room, they hardly were in a position to notice something as insignificant as a pinprick.

It was only possible for a rogue like Matthew Hopkins to operate at a time when there was a power vacuum. Under ordinary circumstances, even in the seventeenth century, anybody employing torture as Hopkins did would have been called to account. Even before the Felton Case, it was universally recognized that torture was an exceptional process in England, one which was only undertaken by the state in the gravest of cases. There was also growing incredulity about some of the statements being made by Matthew Hopkins about evidence which he claimed was irrefutable proof of supernatural activity. One of the first women interrogated by Hopkins and Stearne was an 80-year-old woman with one leg, called Elizabeth Clark. After being kept awake for days, she said that she did indeed have a number of familiar spirits whom she suckled from a secret nipple. They were named Pyewackett, Vinegar Tom and Grizzell Greedigut. To give some idea of the standard of evidence in capital cases involving allegations of witchcraft at this time, we note that Matthew Hopkins was apparently vastly impressed when told the names of Elizabeth Clark's familiars and said that, 'No mortal could invent such a name'. He assured the court that the very names 'Pyewacket' and 'Grizzell Greedigut', were sufficient proof in themselves of diabolical involvement. On such slender evidence was a disabled old woman convicted of witchcraft and hanged.

It is impossible at this late stage to be sure of Matthew Hopkins' motives for riding across Essex, Suffolk and Norfolk, hunting out witches. There can be little doubt that financial considerations played at least some part. At a time when a farm labourer might typically earn 6d (3p) a day, Hopkins was collecting £15 or £20 from each village or town that he visited. As the first phase of the English Civil

War drew to a close in 1646, however, a more regular judicial system began to be re-established and Hopkins was viewed with increasing disfavour. He retired from the witch finding business in 1646 and died of tuberculosis the following year. His career had lasted just eighteen months, but he had achieved immortality of sorts for his innovations in the field of torture.

Hopkins became something of a celebrity in East Anglia, certainly better known than his onetime mentor, John Stearne. Pamphlets were published about his activities, illustrated with woodcuts showing both Hopkins and some of his victims. In Illustration 11, we see Matthew Hopkins, together with two of the 'witches' whom he discovered and sent to the gallows, including Elizabeth Clark and her familiar spirits.

We saw in the Introduction that James Naylor, in addition to having a red-hot spike driven through his tongue, was also branded on the forehead with a letter 'B'. Branding, which surely nobody could deny is torture, was commonly used throughout British history on convicted criminals and even those not found guilty of any offence. Despite the supposed abandonment of torture which was encouraged by Coke, branding with red-hot irons enjoyed a sudden resurgence at the end of the seventeenth century. It proved to be a counterproductive move. Although the motive was to reduce crime, it actually had the opposite effect!

In Tudor England, branding was used on various classes of criminal. Under a statute passed in 1547, vagabonds and gypsies were to be branded on the chest with a 'V' and those who started fights in church with an 'F', standing for 'Fray-maker'. Later in the sixteenth century, political crimes were sometimes punished by a spell in the pillory and being branded on the cheeks with either 'SS', standing for 'sower of sedition' or 'SL', which indicated 'schismatic libeller'. At various times over the next century and a half, branding was used both as a punishment, as in the case of James Naylor, and also to record permanently those who had claimed 'Benefit of Clergy'. This expression might need a little explanation.

The Anglican Church in Britain was jealous of its rights. When a clergyman or monk was accused of a crime, the Church claimed the right to deal with the offender under their own laws, rather than to have him tried in a civil court. This was a leftover relic of the days when the Catholic Church had operated almost as a parallel government in the country. A person who stood accused of a crime could plead 'Benefit of Clergy' when the case reached court and thus evade the justice of the ordinary courts. Because it was difficult to establish for certain who was and was not entitled to claim immunity from the civil law, the custom of Benefit of Clergy became widely misused and turned into something of a racket. During the seventeenth century, the only evidence required that a man was really a clergyman was that he had to be able to read aloud from the Bible! In other words, literacy alone was sufficient to save some offenders from the shadow of the noose.

Something which the courts were determined to put a stop to was anybody claiming Benefit of Clergy more than once. The best way of doing this was thought to be by permanently marking anybody who had escaped justice in this way, so that if he appeared in any other court in the future, it would be plain that he had already used up his chance of wriggling out of a serious charge. Since branding was already in use as a punishment, it was thought that this might come in handy for identifying those who had claimed Benefit of Clergy.

For most of the time that branding was used like this, to show that people had got away from justice once, the hot iron was applied to the either the thumb or palm of the hand. A letter was used which showed what the charge had been, 'T' for theft, 'M' for manslaughter and so on. In Lancaster Castle, still the site of a modern-day crown court, branding equipment is on display, although it has not been used for over 200 years. A metal plate with two hoops to hold the hand open and a branding iron with the letter 'M' at the end are on open display. It was the custom for the person applying the hot iron to hold up the victim's hand for the judge to see, while proclaiming, 'A fair mark!'

A curious by-product of branding on the hand those who had claimed Benefit of Clergy is the practice, still current today in American courts, for those swearing to tell the truth, the whole truth and nothing but the truth, to raise their right hands and turn the hand palm outward for all to see. This began in the days when it was necessary for somebody giving evidence to prove that they were trustworthy and honest. Showing that they had not been branded for claiming Benefit of Clergy was one way of doing this.

By the end of the seventeenth century, there were those in the legal profession who wanted to see a stronger line taken with defendants who misused the tradition of ecclesiastical immunity. By this time, it was vanishingly rare for any actual priest or monk to be in the dock. Those claiming Benefit of Clergy were invariably common criminals looking for a 'Get out of jail free' card. Branding on the hand did not seem to be acting as a deterrent, so why not make things a little more unpleasant for such people? In 1698 a new law was passed, which stated that anybody accused of petty larceny or theft who claimed Benefit of Clergy in the future should be branded not on the hand but, 'burnt in the most visible part of the left cheek, nearest the nose'.

Having a red-hot iron pressed into the face might be expected to discourage even the most desperate from trying to escape the gallows by pretending to be a clergyman, but after only nine years, this law was repealed and branding continued on the hand, rather than the face. The reason had nothing to do with common humanity, but was purely a matter of pragmatism. Those who have read *Les Miserables* or seen the film, will know that after he is freed from the galleys, the protagonist is given identity papers which tell everybody that he has been a dangerous criminal. As a consequence, he is unable to find work or even a place to stay for the night and so becomes a thief. This was precisely the effect of branding a man's face. Those who were marked in this way for all to see could not find work and were denied entry to inns. To quote a contemporary source, which explained why the law was changed a few years later, reinstating branding on the hand, making an obvious scar on the face,

> had not had its desired effect of deterring offenders from the further committing of crimes and offences but, on the contrary, such offenders, being rendered thereby unfit in any service or employment to get their livelihood in any honest and lawful way, became the more desperate.

In short, advertising a man's crime in this way virtually guaranteed that in the future he would only be able to survive by committing more crimes.

Although branding on the hand, and sometimes on the thumb, continued for the rest of the eighteenth century and a decade or so of the nineteenth, it gradually became less severe until its use was chiefly symbolic. The number of offences for which Benefit of Clergy could be claimed had been shrinking for many years and with the development of the so-called 'Bloody Code' in the later eighteenth century, which imposed the death penalty, without Benefit of Clergy, for hundreds of offences, the chances of evading punishment through means of an outdated reverence for the Church, became slender indeed. Even when some minor crime or other fell within the category of those for which Benefit of Clergy could be claimed, the branding was frequently done with an unheated iron. The last case of actual branding with a hot iron was in 1811 and the whole thing was finally abolished in 1822.

We have looked at what was happening in England and Scotland up until the end of the eighteenth century. How did the British attitudes towards torture affect what was happening in the territories which were claimed overseas? In other words, did concern about Magna Carta and various key cases such as that of Felton in 1628 make a difference to the likelihood of torture being used in the colonies? This will be the subject of the next chapter.

Chapter 4

The Early Colonial Period

The early years of Britain's involvement in countries outside Europe was largely a matter of private enterprise. The exploits of men such as Francis Drake are all but indistinguishable from piracy and although cruelty might have been inflicted by such men on the native inhabitants of other countries, this can hardly be classified as judicial torture. The story of torture in the colonies really begins when parts of America, Africa, Asia and Australasia were claimed for the Crown and permanently occupied by British settlers, who attempted to recreate the English and Scottish models of civil society, thousands of miles from their own country.

The one thing which must be borne in mind when considering this aspect of torture is that the white colonists did not regard the indigenous natives as being human. They were therefore viewed as being outside the law. Obviously, in seventeenth-century England, one could not go about mutilating, flogging or even killing one's neighbour without falling foul of the law. The situation was seen as being quite different for a white Englishman living in Jamaica, America or India. In the case of America and the West Indies, those who were not white were not only not fully human, in many cases they were actually owned by white men, as though they were horses or dogs. Just as no farmer would hesitate to brand one of his horses or cows, so too did those who traded in and bought slaves routinely brand them with red-hot irons, as a permanent record of whom they belonged to. This was very handy of course of any slave should attempt to escape. In Illustration 13, we see a female slave being branded in this way. It is plain that those undertaking this terrible action have no concern for the woman being subjected to such agonising pain.

It was the idea that black people were not really human which provided justification for their mistreatment. Some prominent white plantation owners in the Caribbean were explicit about such views and tried to persuade others to share them. Edward Long, for example, owned slaves in Jamaica, who worked on his land. In 1774, he published a book called *History of Jamaica*, in which he analysed the character of black people. According to Long, they were, 'unjust, cruel, barbarous, half-human, treacherous, deceitful, thieves, drunkards, proud, lazy, unclean, shameless, jealous to fury, and cowards'! After such a judgement, it will come as no surprise to read that Long decided that:

When we reflect on the nature of these men, and their dissimilarity to the rest of mankind, must we not conclude that they are of a different species of the same genus?

Cruelty to and torture of black people in the islands of the Caribbean under English rule began almost as soon as the colonization started in the early seventeenth century. By the middle of that century, it was an accepted fact of life. Here is what a priest, Father Antoine Biet, said of the behaviour of the English settlers in Barbados in 1652:

They treat their negro slaves with a great deal of severity. If some go beyond the limits of the plantation on a Sunday they are given fifty blows with a cudgel; these often bruise them severely.

Some of the behaviour towards the black workers was almost inconceivably vicious. Father Biet visited an Irish plantation owner and wrote later:

He had in irons one of those poor negroes who had stolen a pig. Every day, his hands in irons, the overseer had him whipped by the other negroes until he was all covered in blood. The overseer, after having him treated thus for seven or eight days, cut off one of his ears, had it roasted, and forced him to eat it.

It is perhaps difficult to decide if such conduct qualifies as private or judicial torture. Since the law allowed people to be treated in this way by their 'owners', it is a debatable point. Legally, slaves in the Caribbean could be flogged, castrated, have their feet amputated, their ears or noses removed or be subject to any other treatment of the most inhuman and depraved kind. It was not just the 'owners' of slaves who ordered terrible punishments though, this was also done by the administrations of the various islands. There was always the fear in places such as Barbados and Jamaica that because the black people so greatly outnumbered the white, then there might at any time be an uprising. This was not an unfounded apprehension; there were a number of slave revolts, some of them successful. The governments of the islands felt that the only way to keep the black people in subjugation was by the fear of frightful punishments which could be inflicted for the most trifling of reasons.

Montserrat is a Caribbean island which was settled by English and Irish emigrants from the middle of the seventeenth century. The colony of whites was always outnumbered by blacks and this meant that very fierce measures were taken to suppress anything which looked like opposition to white rule. The minutes of the Council and Assembly of Montserrat, the ruling body of the island, recorded in August 1693 some of the punishments handed out to black men who broken the law. A man called Peter Boone had stolen nine pigs and when caught had been hanged, cut down alive and disembowelled. This awful sentence was reserved in England for treason, but it was freely used for theft in the West Indies. Another man was mentioned in the minutes who had attacked an overseer and beaten him. The penalty for this was that he was gibbeted alive, that is to say hung up in chains in a public place and left to die of starvation and thirst. Two years later, the minutes of the General Assembly of Montserrat gave details of a black man who had been convicted of stealing a cow. He was sentenced to be burned alive.

It was not only on the smaller islands that such barbarities were being performed. In 1687 Hans Sloane, who later founded the British Museum, travelled to Jamaica. He catalogued much of the island's flora, but was appalled at the what he saw of the torture of the slaves there. He wrote:

> The punishment for crimes of slaves, are usually for rebellions burning them, by nailing them down with the ground on crooked sticks on every limb, and then applying the fire by degrees from the feet and hands, burning them gradually up to the head, whereby their pains are extravagant. For crimes of a lesser nature gelding, or chopping off half of the foot with an axe.

Gelding, a term more usually applied to livestock on a farm, means simply the removal of the testicles; castration, in other words. It must be recalled that these dreadful acts, the castrations, amputations and deliberately slow burning to death, were not the private pleasures of the 'owners', but rather enacted by the courts.

The behaviour of the whites who ruled the islands of the West Indies, did not improve over the decades and in the eighteenth century reached almost unimaginable heights of beastliness. Not only did the government supress any discontent in the most savage way, individual plantation owners tortured their workers in ways which would seem almost beyond belief, had we not documentary evidence. In one case, we have the diary of a plantation owner, a man who detailed in his own handwriting some of the cruellest behaviour ever meted out by one human to another. Thomas Thistlewood emigrated from England to Jamaica in 1750, when he was 29 years of age. He was to spend the rest of his life there, running a sugar cane plantation. In his diary, Thistlewood was meticulous in recording all his activities, including the 3,852 times that he had sexual intercourse with 138 different women, almost all of them black slaves. It is his methods for keeping order on his estate though which are of particular interest. Readers with delicate sensibilities or who are overly squeamish, would be well advised to skip the next few paragraphs.

The problems that Thomas Thistlewood faced with the slaves on his 160-acre plantation were trivial. They included such things as slaves eating the sugar cane while working and also going missing from time to time and avoiding work. The slaves were given names by Thistlewood to replace their African ones. He called them things such as Egypt, Derby, Hector and Port Royal. On 28 January 1756, Thistlewood noted in his diary his annoyance at finding that one of the slaves had been eating bits of sugar cane. He wrote 'Had Derby well whipped, and made Egypt shit in his mouth'. This practice, of getting one slave to defecate in the mouth of another as a punishment, became a regular event on Thistlewood's plantation and was known as 'Derby's dose'. A few months later on 23 July, a slave ran away and Thistlewood had him flogged and then had lime juice rubbed in the wounds to increase the pain. Then, 'made Hector shit in his mouth, immediately put in a gag whilst his mouth was full & made him wear it 4 or 5 hours'.

To show that these were not isolated instances of torture, we might look at other entries which Thomas Thistlewood made in his diary in July 1756. On 24 July, a female slave was punished by having another slave defecate in her mouth. On Friday, 30 July, a slave called Punch, who had run away, was caught and brought back to Thistlewood's plantation. He wrote:

> Punch catched at Salt River and brought home. Flogged him and Quacoo well and then washed and rubbed in salt pickle, lime juice & bird pepper, also whipped Hector for losing his hoe, made new negro Joe piss in his eyes and mouth &c.

The catalogue of horrors continues, and it would be wearisome just to list all the abuses to which these poor wretches were subjected. Derby, whose punishment gave rise to the general term for the disgusting practice of punishing slaves in this way, was caught stealing corn from a neighbouring plantation. According to Thistlewood's diary, he had Derby's face chopped with a machete, so that his right ear, cheek and jaw were almost cut off.

There is no reason to suppose that Thomas Thistlewood was an especially cruel plantation owner, this is just how things were in the West Indian colonies. Such inhuman treatment, not unnaturally, led to resentment among the slaves and rebellion was never far away. In 1760, just four years after the diary extracts above, a revolt began among the slaves of Jamaica, caused by the harsh conditions under which they were kept. The leader was a recently-arrived African chief, known as Tackey. He led a group of men to the fort at Port Maria, where they killed the sentry and acquired arms and ammunition. There followed a bloody period, during which forty white people were massacred. Vengeance for this was ghastly, when once the rebellion had been put down.

Bryan Edwards, a plantation owner, wrote about the affair. He said that there was a general mood of discontent among many of Jamaica's slaves and that it was decided to make an example of some of the ringleaders of the insurgency;

> Of three who were clearly proved to have been concerned in the murders committed at Ballard's valley, one was condemned to be burnt, and the other two to be hung up alive in irons, and left to perish in that dreadful situation. The wretch that was burnt was made to sit on the ground, and being chained to an iron stake, the fire was applied to his feet. He uttered not a groan, and saw his legs reduced to ashes with the utmost firmness and composure; after which, one of his arms by some means getting loose, he snatched a brand from the fire that was consuming him and flung it in the face of the executioner.
>
> The two that were hung up alive were indulged, at their own request, with a hearty meal immediately before they were suspended on the gibbet, which was erected in the parade of the town of Kingston. From that time, until they expired, they never uttered the least complaint, except only of cold in the night, but diverted themselves all day long in discourse with their countrymen, who were permitted, most improperly, to surround the gibbet.

The two men who were gibbetted alive took over a week to die. It was by such means, torturing those who took part to death, that the British hold over colonies such as Jamaica was maintained.

Gibbetting alive might be an unfamiliar concept to many readers, who may have the idea that gibbets were something like the gallows. In fact, gibbets were, in the usual way of things, a means of displaying corpses, this being done to deter others from following the same path which brought the dead men to such a fate. Gibbeting was done by enclosing the dead body of an executed criminal with bands of iron and then hanging it up in a prominent place, often until it fell to pieces. Gibbetting alive meant hammering iron straps around a living man and then hanging him up to die of thirst, starvation and exposure. A person gibbetted alive is shown in Illustration 13. The horror of being enclosed in iron bands in this way and simply left to die, is almost beyond imagining.

The two cases above of gibbetting alive in the West Indies were not all that unusual. A nineteenth-century magazine, *Once a Week,* published an article about a set of gibbetting irons which had been found in Jamaica. They had been made for gibbetting alive. The magazine said:

> Round the knees, hips and waist, under the arms and around the neck, iron hoops were rivetted close about the different parts of the body. Iron

braces crossed these again, from the hips right over the centre of the head. Iron plates and bars encircled and supported the legs, and at the lower extremities were fixed plates of iron like old fashioned stirrups, in which the feet might have found rest, had not a finish to the torture, compared to which crucifixion itself must have been mild, been contrived by fixing in each stirrup three sharp-pointed spikes to pierce the soles of the victim's feet. The only support the body could receive, while strength remained or life endured, was given by a narrow hoop passing from one end of the waist bar in front between the legs to the bar at the back. Attached to the circular band under the arms, stood out a pair of handcuffs, which prevented the slightest motion in the hands; and on the crossing of the hoops over the head was a strong hook, by which the whole fabric, with the sufferer enclosed, was suspended.

A more ghastly death can hardly be imagined: the person could easily linger on for days in this terrible torment. There is no doubt that black people in the Caribbean under British rule were treated with great cruelty; tortured and killed at the whim of owners or the courts. They had very little protection under the law.

There was of course a glaring anomaly here and it was one of which the British public were increasingly aware. On the one hand, the fiction was being propagated that the British colonization of various hot countries was a good and desirable thing for the native population. These savages were being brought under the rule of law and taught how to comport themselves like civilized beings. They were reaping all the benefits of Magna Carta and learning about British values. On the other hand, the British were killing them in the most ingenious ways that could be devised, as well as mutilating, flogging and starving them whenever it was felt necessary. Torture had been declared illegal in England for almost 200 years and yet here it was being practised freely by English authorities abroad! Something was wrong.

The way that the islands of the Caribbean were being governed by the British, and the use of torture there against suspects, became a cause célèbre in Britain in 1803, with the arrest in London of Brigadier General Thomas Picton, the former governor of Trinidad. He was charged with having carried out summary executions on the island and also with ordering the use of torture against suspected criminals. That the case which was eventually focussed on was that of a 14-year-old girl guaranteed public interest.

Picton was a career soldier who fought extensively around the world in the Napoleonic wars. In the late eighteenth century, he commanded forces which attacked the Caribbean islands of St Vincent and St Lucia and after their capture from Spain, he was appointed governor of Trinidad. For the next five years, Picton ruled the island as though it were his own personal fiefdom, dealing out torture and execution at whim. He was later to be charged with twenty-nine counts of death 'unlawfully inflicted', to use the legal phrase. These included hangings, beheadings and men burned alive. Much of the torture concerned alleged cases of witchcraft, which Picton seemed to take very seriously. It should be noted that the facts of what happened while Thomas Picton governed Trinidad were never really in dispute. The whole affair boiled down to the legality or otherwise of his actions. The executions and torture were, after all, not really remarkable when considered in the context of the general behaviour of the white rulers of the West Indies at that time.

Even by prevailing standards, Picton's excesses were raising eyebrows in London by 1802 and it was decided that it might be wise to rein him in a bit. Instead of being sole governor of Trinidad, he would in future be just one of three commissioners. This did not suit the autocratic Picton and he resigned, returning to London where, in 1803, he was arrested. Bail was set at the astoundingly high sum of £40,000, equivalent today to perhaps £3,000,000. This was some indication of how seriously the offences were regarded by the establishment in London.

To begin with, the various deaths were dealt with, but the prosecution soon found itself bogged down in the finer points of international law. Trinidad had been a Spanish possession, administered according to Spanish law, and Picton was able to demonstrate that when appointed, he had been instructed to continue applying Spanish law rather than English law. Since Spanish law permitted torture, this looked like a solid defence against some of the charges. He also invoked military law and claimed that because he was operating at time of war, summary executions were a regrettable necessity. The only charge which was proceeded with was that he had ordered the torture of a girl called Louisa Calderon, who was suspected of complicity in the theft of £500.

Louisa Calderon had, at the age of 11, become the mistress of a man called Pedro Ruiz. It is possible that she took another lover a short time later, a man called Carlos Gonzalez. That at least is what Ruiz believed and, perhaps in a spirit of revenge, he then made a formal accusation to the authorities, claiming that Gonzalez and Calderon had conspired together and stolen £500 from his shop. The theft of such a large sum of money was a capital offence, meaning that anybody convicted of it would face the gallows. Neither Carlos Gonzalez nor Louisa Calderon, though, would admit to having anything to do with the matter and so Calderon was brought before the governor of Trinidad, Thomas Picton himself. He questioned her, but she still refused to confess. Picton had her sent to the island's chief magistrate, St Hilaire Begorrat, who was by way of being a close friend of his. Calderon and Gonzalez though stubbornly maintained their innocence and the jailer of the prison where she was being held sent word to Picton, asking what should be done to the young girl. Calderon was at most 14 years of age at this time and may even have been younger. Picton replied in Spanish, saying, 'Apliquese la questiona Louisa Calderon', which, being freely translated from the demotic, means, 'Apply the torture to Louisa Calderon'.

The type of torture used on the girl was a variation of the punishment known in the Spanish army as the 'piquet'. Her right hand was bound to her left foot and she was hoisted into the air by a rope tied around her left wrist. The only support provided for her right foot was a pointed wooden stake. The strain of being suspended in this way by one wrist was terrific, and any attempt to alleviate the discomfort meant trying to support the weight of the body on the sharp stake. It was a fiendish torment, which Louisa Calderon was compelled to undergo for an hour. The following day, she was subjected once more to the piquet, this time for a little over twenty minutes. Still, she refused to confess and so Picton had her confined to a cell for eight months, constantly shackled in irons. No charge was ever brought against her and she was not brought to court. It was this case which captivated London in 1806, when Thomas Picton was brought to trial at the King's Bench.

The case of the tortured teenage girl captivated London and illustrators vied with each other to see which could provide the most titillating images of the young girl's suffering. An example of the contemporary artwork inspired by the case may be seen in Illustration 14. When Louisa herself was brought to London to give evidence, she became a celebrity overnight. The fact that she was attractive and personable did not help Picton at his trial. There was no doubt that the young woman still had scars on her wrists and she gave her evidence in a most convincing way. Thomas Picton was convicted, but immediately appealed, pending which he was again released on bail. The end of the affair will surprise nobody, considering that on the one hand was a penniless, young black woman and on the other a high-ranking British Army officer. The verdict was reversed and Picton was set free. He was later killed at the Battle of Waterloo.

Before leaving the subject of torture as used in the first British colonies, we must look at the only officially sanctioned case of torture to be used in America when it was under British control. It is true that people, principally black slaves and Native Americans, were being mistreated and even killed unofficially in America during the seventeenth and eighteenth centuries, but that was all extra-judicial. Only one instance is known where torture was applied legally and by order of the courts, in order to make a man say or do something.

The village of Salem was a community of Puritans in the British colony of Massachusetts. It was a devout and God-fearing society, where Christian faith of a particularly strict kind was practised. In the spring of 1692 a number of young girls began to display signs of hysteria, claiming that they had been bewitched. One of the first to exhibit these symptoms was 9-year-old Elizabeth Parris, daughter of the Reverend Samuel Parris. By May, the situation in Salem was at fever-pitch, with various girls ranging in age from 9 to 19 accusing people in the village of having caused them to become possessed. The Governor of Massachusetts, Sir William Phips, set up a special court to investigate the allegations being made by the girls. There was every incentive for those accused of witchcraft to confess, because those doing so were able to give evidence themselves and were freed from the threat of prosecution. Some people, however, refused to cooperate in the farce.

There were some who preferred to face the prospect of hanging rather than perjure themselves by stating under oath that they had been practising magic, when they all knew very well that they had not. One man, 72-year-old George Jacobs, was accused by his own granddaughter of being a wizard and brought to trial. In court, he said angrily to the judges, 'You tax me for a wizard? You may as well tax me for a buzzard!' His defiance did him no good, for on 19 August 1692, he was hanged. Somebody else who would not play the game was a very pious old woman called Martha Corey. She had expressed the view that there were no such things as witches and that the girls were simply making up stories. Inevitably, when some of the children got to hear of this, they accused Martha Corey herself of bewitching them. During her trial, two of the girls told the court that they could see the devil whispering in her ear. Such 'spectral evidence' was sufficient for the jury to convict her and she too was hanged, like eighteen others.

In April that year, Martha Corey's husband Giles had been arrested and taken to prison. This was done after a teenage girl called Mercy Lewis swore the following statement:

> I saw the Apparition of Giles Corey come and afflict me urging me to write in his book and so he continued most dreadfully to hurt me by times beating me & almost breaking my back tell the day of his examination being the 19th of April and then also during the time of his examination he did affect and tortor me most greviously: and also several times sense urging me vehemently to write in his book and I veryly believe in my heart that Giles Corey is a dreadful wizard for sense he had been in prison he or his appearance has come and most greviously tormented me.

When he was brought to court in September to face the charge of witchcraft, Giles Corey refused point-blank to have anything to do with the proceedings. The 81-year-old man would not even plead 'guilty' or 'not guilty' to the indictment. English law allowed of course for those refusing to enter a plea to be subjected to the terrible torture known as the *Peine Forte et Dure*. This had never been used in the American colonies, however, and there was some uncertainty about how to proceed. Corey was taken back to prison and brought before the court once more, when he again refused to plead. It was decided that the only correct course of action was to put him to the *Peine Forte et Dure*. As a matter of fact, the very sentence passed in this case was illegal, for two reasons. First, although widely used in England, the Commonwealth of Massachusetts had no law prescribing this procedure on its statute book. Not only that, it violated the Puritans' own code, the Body of Liberties, which proscribed barbarous treatment. On any reading of the law, pressing to death was an unlawful act. During hysterical times such as witch hunts though, we might expect such minor points of law to be overlooked and so it proved in this case.

Giles Corey had a very strong motive for not wishing to be convicted of witchcraft. He had extensive property, consisting of both buildings and land, and wanted to make sure that his relatives retained this, rather than its being seized by the state. This is what would have happened had he been convicted of a capital crime. So it was that on 18 September 1692 the old man was led to a field next to the town gaol, stripped and spreadeagled on the ground, his ankles and wrists being tied to four posts which had been driven into the ground. Then a stout board was placed on his chest and six men piled heavy rocks on the boards. Although in England, the *Peine Forte et Dure* had effectively evolved into a way of putting a man to death, the authorities in Salem decided to treat the traditional sentence literally and follow the instructions to the very letter. For instance, it will be recalled that the original sentence called for the victim to be given bread on the second day and bread and water thereafter each day that he refused to plead. The sentence passed on Giles Corey at Salem included the words that he should be:

> laid on his back on the bare floor, naked, unless when decency forbids;
> that there be placed upon his body as great a weight as he could bear, and
> more, that he hath no sustenance, save only on the first day, three morsels
> of the worst bread, and the second day three draughts of standing water,
> that should be alternately his daily diet till he died, or, till he answered.

The day after Giles Corey was laid out with the terrible weight upon his chest, he was given three small pieces of bread, which he ate. On the second day, after forty-eight hours of the most excruciating torture, the judges and the sheriff came to visit him and see if he had changed his mind. When asked if he was ready yet to plead, he responded only by saying, 'More weight!' More heavy rocks were indeed added to the weight which was already crushing him. A bystander, Robert Calef, later wrote that, 'In the pressing, Giles Corey's tongue was pressed out of his mouth, the Sheriff, with his cane, forced it in again.' The words 'more weight' were the last that Corey was ever to speak, because a short while later, he died. One of the judges who was present, Samuel Sewall, recorded in his diary that,

> About noon at Salem, Giles Cory [*sic*] was pressed to death for standing mute; much pains was used with him two days, one after another, by the court and Captain Gardner of Nantucket who had been of his acquaintance, but all in Vain.

The pressing to death of Giles Corey was the only case known of the official use of torture in the American colonies. There was certainly informal use of torture by settlers, principally on black slaves and native Americans, but the case at Salem was the only time that a court had ordered anything of the kind.

Of course, just as in the islands of the Caribbean under British rule, slavery was practised in America, and indeed, lingered on there until the end of the American Civil War in 1865. Slavery entailed a good deal of torture, including such routine cruelty as the branding of men, women and children like cattle to establish ownership and was widespread during the period when America consisted of British colonies. Black slaves could be mistreated and even killed, without any serious consequences for the 'owners'. In effect, the slaves were treated virtually as domestic animals. An example of this dreadful attitude may be seen when, in 1669, the Assembly of Virginia endorsed the idea that if a slave was being physically punished by his or her owner and, 'by the extremity of his correction should chance to die', then this would not be regarded as a felony. South Carolina too passed a law which stated clearly that an owner should have 'absolute power and authority over his negro slaves'. It need hardly be added that being given a free hand in this way led to many abuses and not a few deaths.

Slaves in British colonies, both in the Caribbean and on the American mainland, could be whipped, branded, mutilated and even killed with impunity by those who supposedly owned them. Such barbarous treatment was not seen by most people in Britain as torture, any more than applying a whip to a horse was thought to be. When humans are classified both legally and in the opinion of most people as no more than animals, then usual consideration cease to apply. Animals are routinely castrated on farms and the same procedure was undertaken on slaves without its causing any raised eyebrows. This casual racism was endemic throughout the British Empire for centuries and meant that those from Africa, Asia and America could be subjected to tortures of such a nature as would cause horror and loathing, were they to be inflicted upon a white person. We will deal in greater detail with this in the chapter on the British Empire.

We have looked so far a torture which, while causing severe pain, is not usually a threat to life. Of course, the *Peine Forte et Dure* was often fatal, but this was usually a consequence of the person undergoing it refusing to speak. One way in which torture was in regular use without anybody raising their eyebrows and thinking anything of it was during public executions. In those cases, the general view was that the more pain which was suffered, the better example would the execution be to the onlookers. In the next chapter, we shall examine some of the methods of capital punishment which had been deliberately devised to cause as much pain as possible.

Chapter 5

Tortured to Death: Deliberately Prolonged Suffering in Executions

In much of the modern world, the death penalty has fallen into abeyance. In countries which do still carry out executions, they are in general conducted as expeditiously and painlessly as possible. The purpose is to dispose of the prisoner with the minimum amount of fuss or suffering. If a condemned person suffers any pain during the execution, this is regarded as needless cruelty. However, this way of doing things is a fairly recent development in penological theory. For almost the whole of recorded history, the idea has been to make the death of condemned criminals as slow, gory and painful as could be. In Britain, prolonged and agonising deaths, combined with mass executions, were thought until the nineteenth century to be the most effective way of deterring crime. Of course, this is not the case. It is the likelihood of being detected and apprehended which discourages criminals, not the type or severity of the penalty. If there is an outstandingly good chance of getting away with stealing or murder, then people will be more inclined to commit these crimes.

In England, during the Medieval and Tudor periods, it was taken as axiomatic that frightful deaths would put the fear of God into men and women and ensure that they obeyed the law. Sometimes, more than usually dreadful executions were staged, in the hope that those watching would take notice and be deterred from committing such crimes themselves. Take the case of Richard Rouse, who was executed at Smithfield in London in 1531. Rouse, or Rice, Roose or Rose - nobody knows how he wished his name to be spelled - was one of the cooks at the Bishop of Rochester's palace. The bishop, John Fisher, was not popular with the king, Henry VIII, which later gave rise to rumours that he himself was somehow associated with what happened. On 18 February 1531, Rouse put something into the pot of gruel being prepared for the bishop's evening meal. Fortunately for Bishop Fisher, he wasn't feeling hungry that day and directed that the food which had been prepared should be given to the servants and also any beggars in the vicinity. This was done and more than a dozen of those who ate the gruel fell ill. Two of them, Bennett Curwen and Alice Tryppyt, died. Richard Rouse admitted at once what he had done and claimed that it had been by way of a practical joke, that he thought the stuff he put in the gruel was merely a laxative.

Poisoning has always been seen as worse than other methods of murder. Even to this day, in cases of murder by poisoning, it is customary for the Attorney General to conduct the prosecution in person. Rouse was not even given a trial. Henry VIII passed an Act of Attainder, not only declaring the cook guilty, but also prescribing a new and terrible punishment for such crimes. The 1531 Acte for Poysoning begins:

> On the Eighteenth day of February, 1531, one Richard Roose, of Rochester, cook, also called Richard Cooke, did cast poison into a vessel of yeast to baum, standing in the kitchen of the Bishop of Rochester's Palace, at Lambeth March, by means of which two persons who happened to eat of the pottage made with such yeast died.

The penalty for poisoning now prescribed, and to be enforced retroactively, was boiling alive. Perhaps this was some fiendish piece of humour on the king's part. The cook had put poison in a cauldron over a fire; now he was himself to die in a cauldron.

Richard Rouse was executed at Smithfield, where those burned at the stake were traditionally disposed of. On 5 April 1531, Rouse was led to the huge cauldron in which he would die. It was intended that his execution should be protracted, though, and so he was not just cast into the boiling water to die at once. Instead, according to a contemporary record, the spelling of which has been tidied up a little;

> This year was a cook boiled in a cauldron in Smithfield for he would have poisoned the bishop of Rochester Fisher with diverse of his servants, and he was locked in a chain and pulled up and down with a gibbet at diverse times till he was dead.

Rouse was dipped in the hot water and then swiftly drawn out again, allowed to recover a little and then lowered again, before being taken out again. The execution lasted for a long time. Even by the sensibilities of sixteenth-century England, a time far less sensitive and squeamish than our own, this was felt to be a bit much. An eyewitness related that:

> He roared mighty loud, and diverse women who were big with child did feel sick at the sight of what they saw, and were carried away half dead; and other men and women did not seem frightened by the boiling alive, but would prefer to see the headsman at his work.

There are only two other known cases of this excruciatingly painful technique being used. The first was a maidservant who was executed in the Norfolk town of King's Lynn in the same year that Richard Rouse died. She too was dipped repeatedly in the boiling water until she was dead. The other case was a woman called Margaret Davy, who was boiled alive at Smithfield on 28 March 1542. When Henry VIII died in 1547, his son Edward repealed the law.

Despite there only having been three executions by boiling alive, something about the business caught the public imagination and a new nickname was coined for the public executioner. For the rest of the sixteenth century, executioners were referred to by the general name of 'William Boilman'. Dreadful as such deaths were to witness, the novelty value made them memorable.

Boiling to death was certainly a ghastly way to die, but even some of the commoner ways of executing criminals could be tweaked to make them last longer and so increase the pain felt before death supervened. Take burning alive, for example, a popular-enough method of execution in Tudor England. Now as a rule, being burned at the stake tended to be a pretty swift death. The commonest way for somebody being executed in this way to die was by inhaling carbon monoxide and so being asphyxiated. Failing that, breathing in the extremely hot air from the fire often caused the airways to swell up, leading to the victim choking to death, which might have been unpleasant, but was at least quick.

Sometimes, however, it was thought desirable for those being burned alive to suffer a more than usually unpleasant death. Just as the execution could be speeded up by strangling the condemned person before the flames were even lit, so too could it be prolonged. This was sometimes done with heretics who, it was thought, deserved a foretaste of the burning torment which they would soon be suffering in the afterlife. Two instances of this will serve to illustrate the point.

We are all of us familiar with Sir John Falstaff, the merry drunkard from Shakespeare's play *Henry V*. Falstaff was based upon a friend of the real Henry V, whose name was Sir John Oldcastle. In early edition of the play, he is called Oldcastle and not Falstaff. His descendants objected and so Shakespeare changed the name. Oldcastle was a good friend of Henry V until they fell out over religion. Henry was an orthodox and zealous Catholic, whereas Sir John Oldcastle became a Lollard, an early form of Protestant. The result was that Oldcastle was tried for heresy and convicted. He escaped from the Tower of London and it was to be four years before he was captured and the sentence of burning alive carried out. It had been decided to make an example of Sir John Oldcastle and when he was taken to be executed at St Giles Fields, roughly where the present-day Charing Cross Road meets Oxford Street and Tottenham Court Road, a special arrangement had been made. Oldcastle was to be roasted over a slow fire. This was done by suspending him in chains above the fire and ensuring that it was not fierce enough to kill him in a hurry. This execution may be seen in Illustration 15.

An even slower death was contrived for John Forest, a priest who was unwise enough to speak out from the pulpit of St Paul's Cathedral against Henry VIII's plan to divorce Catherine of Aragon and marry Anne Boleyn. This was around the same time that the king was supressing monastic orders and he was in no mood to brook any opposition. But Forest, who was later beatified by the Catholic Church, was not a man who feared to take a stand. He refused to accept Henry VIII as supreme head of the church in England and nor would he moderate his views on the king's divorce. Forest was condemned to death and on 22 May 1538 was taken to Smithfield to be executed. A very high gibbet had been erected and from this, John Forest was hanged in chains, high above the pile of wood which was to be used to burn him. So high was he suspended and so slowly was the fire stoked, that it took an almost unbelievable two hours for the priest to die.

Of course, even without these extra refinements, burning at the stake could be a grim business. Take the death of John Hooper in 1555. Hooper was the Bishop of Worcester and Gloucester under Henry VIII. As an Anglican, he fell foul of Henry's daughter Mary, who was fiercely Catholic. When she became queen in 1553, following the death of her brother Edward VI, Mary set about persecuting anybody who failed to acknowledge Catholicism as the one true faith. The former bishop was tried for heresy and, on 9 February 1555, burned at the stake. He died hard, as they said in those days. The day of Hooper's execution was a cold one and the bundles of reeds which were used for the fire were green, which meant that they burned poorly. Hooper was not at all worried about being executed, being convinced that he was dying a martyr for the faith in which he fervently believed. He told the executioner that it would not be necessary to bind him to the stake, but was content to allow a metal band to be placed around his waist and secured to the stake. His death is described in gruesome detail in *Foxe's Book of Martyrs*:

> But because there were put to no fewer green faggots than two horses could carry upon their backs, it kindled not by and by, and was a pretty while also before it took the reeds upon the faggots. At length it burned about him, but the wind having full strength in that place, (it was a lowering and cold morning), it blew the flame from him, so that he was in a manner no more but touched by the fire.
>
> Within a space after, a few dry faggots were brought, and a new fire kindled with faggots, (for there were no more reeds), and that burned at the nether parts, but had small power above, because of the wind, saving that it did burn his hair, and scorch his skin a little. In the time of which fire, even as at the first flame, he prayed, saying mildly and not very loud, (but as one without pains), 'Oh Jesus, the Son of David, have mercy upon me, and receive my soul!' After the second was spent, he did wipe both his

eyes with his hands, and beholding the people, he said with an indifferent loud voice, 'For God's love, good people, let me have more fire!' And all this while his nether parts did burn; for the faggots were so few, that the flame did not burn strongly at his upper parts.

The third fire was kindled within a while, which was more extreme than the other two . . . In the which fire he prayed with somewhat of a loud voice, 'Lord Jesus have mercy upon me; Lord Jesus have mercy upon me; Lord Jesus receive my spirit!' And these were the last words he was heard to utter. But when he was black in the mouth, and his tongue swollen, that he could not speak, yet his lips went till they were shrunk to the gums: and he knocked his breast with his hands, until one of his arms fell off, and then knocked still with the other, what time the fat, water, and blood, dropped out at his finger's ends, until by renewing of the fire his strength was gone, and his hand did cleave fast, in knocking, to the iron upon his breast. So immediately, bowing forwards, he yielded up his spirit.

Thus was he three quarters of an hour or more in the fire. Even as a lamb, patiently he abode the extremity thereof, neither moving forwards, backwards, nor to any side: but having his nether parts burned, and his bowels fallen out, he died as quietly as a child in his bed.

By which it may be seen that even an 'ordinary' burning at the stake, with no additional refinement of cruelty or effort to extend the agony, could be described as being tortured to death.

After the end of the sixteenth century, only women were burned at the stake in this way, and then only for treason, never, in England, for witchcraft. Treason though, included not just the most obvious category of those who conspired against the Crown, but also anybody guilty of forging coinage. Women were being burned at the stake for this offence until as late as 1789, although they were invariably strangled before being burned. The last case of anybody being burned alive in England, with all the horrors which that entailed, was the execution of Elizabeth Gaunt in 1685.

Elizabeth Gaunt was a very religious woman, who always helped anybody who asked for her assistance. In 1683, she sheltered and fed a desperate man by the name of James Burton. She wasn't to know it, but Burton was fleeing the country after being mixed up in the Rye House Plot to kill King Charles II and his brother the Duke of York. Two years later, James Burton was caught and, to save his own skin, he promised to tell the authorities about all who had helped him. In exchange for this, he received a pardon. One of those he named was Elizabeth Gaunt. The middle-aged woman was arrested and tried in London for treason. She was sentenced to death by burning, but it was widely expected that a reprieve would be forthcoming. It was not. By the time she was tried in 1685, the Duke of York had become James II, King of England, and he was a vindictive man. The sentence was to stand. On 23 October 1685, Elizabeth Gaunt was burned alive in London, her only crime being to provide charitable aid to a starving man. She bore her misfortune with great stoicism, buoyed up by her deep religious faith. She was an Anabaptist, which might also have been a reason for the Catholic James II to deny her mercy. Witnesses at her execution said that she was cheerful and composed. David Hume, in his *History of England,* describes her death:

> One of the rebels, knowing her humane disposition, had recourse to her in distress and was concealed by her. Hearing of the proclamation which offered an indemnity to such as discovered criminals, he betrayed his benefactress and bore evidence against her. He received a pardon as a recompense for his treachery and she was burnt alive for her charity.

One of the witnesses of her death was William Penn, who related that 'when she had calmly disposed the straw about her in such a manner as to shorten her sufferings, all the bystanders burst into tears'.

The punishment of burning alive, used on women who had been found guilty of treason, was actually designed to be an act of mercy! The penalty for men convicted of treason was of course to be hanged, drawn and quartered and it was felt that such a public display of a woman's body would be indecent. Better by far to burn her, without the mutilations of the naked body prescribed for male traitors. The ritual of hanging, drawing and quartering must surely rank as one of the most painful and disgusting ways that criminals were ever despatched in Britain and the entire process, from beginning to end, was directed towards one single purpose, to make the death of the victim as painful and humiliating as could be.

One of the first people in England to be hanged, drawn and quartered was the Scottish rebel, William Wallace. The actual sentence had not been precisely formulated at that time, in 1305, and this was very much an ad hoc affair, simply to make sure that the condemned man suffered as much as he could. By the time of the Tudors, the whole business of being hanged, drawn and quartered was regulated exactly and described in detail by the sentence pronounced against the man convicted of treason. Judges at the time of Henry VIII, told those about to die;

> That you be drawn on a hurdle to the place of execution where you shall be hanged by the neck and being alive cut down, your privy members shall be cut off and your bowels taken out and burned before you, your head severed from your body and your body divided into four quarters to be disposed of at the king's pleasure.

Each part of the sentence was recommended for particular reasons. The first men to suffer death in this way had simply been dragged to Tyburn behind a horse, their heads bumping and banging on the cobbles as they went. On more than one occasion, the victim had been thus knocked unconscious before the butchery even began, which rather defeated the object of the exercise. The castration was to show that here was a man unworthy of begetting children and the bowels were once thought to be the seat of reason, rather than the head. It was here that the treasonous thoughts must have originated and so it was only fitting that they should be burned. As for dragging the condemned man to his death, his face low to the ground, this was because he had forfeited the right to enjoy the same fresh air as decent people. An example of hanging, drawing and quartering is shown in Illustration 16. This shows Hugh Despenser suffering this fate in the early fourteenth century.

One of the features of this kind of execution was that it could be made either extremely painful and drawn-out or, on the other hand, it could be performed relatively swiftly, with little suffering. It all depended on how long the subject was allowed to hang for before the bodily mutilations began. Hanging, with its pressure on the carotid artery which supplies blood to the brain, can cause unconsciousness in a matter of seconds and some of those who were hanged, drawn and quartered were allowed to hang for so long that they were dead before being taken to the block to be butchered. Sometimes, the executioner would be guided by the mood of the crowd and allow a man to hang long enough before being cut down that he would not experience the horrors of being cut to pieces while alive. At other times though, instructions were received from above that the execution was to be as hideous as could be contrived. Sometimes this could backfire and create sympathy for those being tortured so dreadfully. This happened in 1586, when a group of Catholics conspired to have Elizabeth I overthrown and her cousin Mary Queen of Scots installed as Queen of England in her place. This became known to history as the Babington Plot.

The principal figures in the Babington Plot were the 24-year-old Anthony Babington, a Catholic nobleman, and a priest called John Ballard. There could hardly have been a worse or more clear-cut case of treason, with discussions taking place within the group and by means of correspondence with Mary Queen of Scots, about assassinating Elizabeth, inviting the Spanish to occupy England and seeing Mary take the throne. It is little wonder that Elizabeth was absolutely furious to discover such treachery in her realm.

During the trial of the fourteen conspirators, Queen Elizabeth spoke privately to William Cecil, Baron Burghley, asking if it would be possible to devise a new and more painful way of executing these traitors. Writing later to Sir Christopher Hatton, Cecil said that the queen had told him that she thought that existing methods of capital punishment were too mild for such a shocking case of treason. This was of course a most improper thing to do, since Burghley was one of the commissioners trying the case and Babington and the others had not, at that point, even been found guilty. Nevertheless, he assured the queen that when done correctly, hanging, drawing and quartering was the most fearsome means of execution in all the world. So it proved, when the first batch of seven plotters, having been convicted of treason, were brought to St Giles' Field on 20 September 1586, to expiate their crime.

It was obvious from the beginning that the executioner had been told to make death as hard as could be for the seven men being put to death that day. The first to die was the priest, John Ballard. He was hoisted in the air for a very short time and then immediately lowered back to the scaffold. Ballard was given time to recover and catch his breath before the main part of the execution took place. He was stripped naked and his penis and testicles sliced off. There was then a pause, before the executioner slit open the suffering man's stomach and carefully removed his intestines. These were then burnt in front of him on a brazier that had been set up on the scaffold. After another pause, his head was removed and his body hacked into four pieces. The other six men were compelled to watch this performance, while they awaited their own turn.

This exhibition of cruelty did not appeal to the crowd, who could see that instructions had been issued that these men were to be treated as barbarously as could be managed. One witness that day was William Camden, who wrote that the men were 'Hanged, cut down, their privities cut off, bowelled alive and seeing, and quartered, not without some note of cruelty'. That they were 'bowelled alive and seeing' tells us plainly that these men were all fully conscious of what was being done to them. For a spectator at a sixteenth-century execution to observe that the proceedings took place 'not without some note of cruelty' is very revealing. Executions were cruel affairs, that was after all the point of them. That Camden remarked on the cruelty at this one meant that it was more than usually dreadful. The reaction of the crowd to what had been done to Anthony Babington and his companions was reported back to the queen and she, ever sensitive to public opinion, gave orders that the second batch of plotters, due to die the following day, should all be left to hang until they were dead. Creating sympathy for the plotters would have been counterproductive.

Hanging, drawing and quartering was, even without any special efforts, a very hit-and-miss business, with some victims being slowly tortured to death and other dying fairly easily on the gallows. The element of chance depended, among other things, on the quality of the rope used for the hanging and the fickle mood of the spectators. The wave of executions which took place after the Gunpowder Plot shows both these aspects of the process in action.

On 31 January 1606, the last two of the Gunpowder Plotters to be executed in Westminster Palace yard were Robert Keyes and Guy Fawkes himself. Most of those who had already been hanged, drawn and quartered for their part in the attempt to blow up Parliament had suffered greatly, being cut down from the gallows after only swinging for a second or two. In Keyes, case, he did not hang at all. As soon as he was off the ladder and the rope took his weight, it snapped at once. He was carried immediately to the block and was dismembered while completely conscious and aware of what was being done to him.

One of the Catholic priests suspected of being connected with the Gunpowder Plot had a very different experience. Father Henry Garnet was executed on 3 May, four months after Guy Fawkes and the rest. Perhaps the public mood had changed in the intervening months. There had been little sympathy for the men who were executed earlier in the year, now though the appetite for vengeance seemed to be ebbing. As soon as Father Garnet had been turned off the ladder, the executioner showed signs of being about to cut him down, but the watching crowd would have none of it. They surged forward and there were cries of, 'Hold, hold!' Not only would they not let the hangman begin work on the priest's body while he was alive, they took active steps to shorten his ordeal. Some hung on Garnet's legs to hasten his death, an office usually performed by the relatives of a condemned person. By the time the executioner was able to take down Father Garnet, he was quite dead.

The sentence of hanging, drawing and quartering was gradually amended in practice over the next sixty years or so, in that the victims were invariably left hanging until they were dead. An exception was made after the restoration of the monarchy, following Charles I's beheading and the republic led by Oliver Cromwell. When Charles II came to the throne in 1660, an amnesty was declared for almost everybody, other than those who had had a direct hand in the death of his father. There followed a series of executions of the most traditional kind, in which the men were taken down from the gallows after a short time and then allowed to recover before they were castrated and disembowelled. Samuel Pepys wrote in his diary in October 1660 of going to watch one of these old-style executions:

To my Lord's in the morning, where I met with Captain Cuttance, but my Lord not being up I went to Charing Cross, to see Major General Harrison hanged, drawn and quartered; which was done there, he looking as cheerful as any man could do in that situation. He was presently cut down, and his head and heart shown to the people, at which there were great shouts of joy.

These were the last traditional executions of this type to take place, where those being cut open were alive and conscious. It is likely that the executioner was told to ensure that this was the case, a special mark of detestation of those who had taken the life of a king.

Burning, boiling alive and hanging, drawing and quartering were all executions which were specifically intended to cause extreme suffering. They were meant to involve men and women being tortured to death, as this was supposed to be a wholesome sight for anybody minded to commit similar crimes. Even when the method of execution was supposed to be as painless and dignified as could be; things could go wrong and entail enormous suffering. Take beheading.

Having one's head removed from the body with one swift cut of a sharp axe is probably one of the quickest ways to kill anybody. The blood rushed out of the body, the brain is deprived of oxygen and death will, under ideal circumstances, be all but instantaneous. Of course, cutting off the head of somebody with an axe and block relies to a great extent upon the willing cooperation of the condemned person. At the very least, he or she must be prepared to place the neck in the hollowed-out portion of the block and then lay perfectly still, waiting for the axe to fall. Most noblemen and women knew what was expected of them and played their part. It was, after all, in their own interests for the execution to go smoothly and for the headsman to be able to undertake his task without being distracted. When this did not happen, the resulting scenes could be the stuff of nightmares.

When Henry VIII fell out with the Catholic Church, some English clergy fled to the continent, where they were able to denounce the king's actions openly. One who did so was Cardinal Pole. Unfortunately, the cardinal's mother, the Countess of Salisbury, remined in England and the king decided that if he couldn't get hold of Cardinal Pole and chop off his head, then the next best thing would be to take his mother and decapitate her instead. That the woman was 68 and quite innocent, did not apparently bother Henry VIII. The day of the execution was a memorable one. The Countess was imprisoned in the Tower of London for two and a half years before being beheaded and on the wall of her cell, she scratched the following poem:

> For traitors on the block should die;
> I am no traitor, no, not I!
> My faithfulness stands fast and so,
> Towards the block I shall not go!
> Nor make one step, as you shall see;
> Christ in Thy Mercy, save Thou me!

When Margaret Pole was led to the scaffold at the Tower of London, on the morning of 27 May 1541, she refused point-blank to kneel down and put her neck on the block or otherwise cooperate in her own execution. According to the ambassador of the Holy Roman Emperor, who was present and wrote a report on the execution, 'at first, when the sentence of death was made known to her, she found the thing very strange, not knowing of what crime she was accused, nor how she had been sentenced'. The overall impression gained was that the countess was confused and did not really understand what was going on. Given her age, it is possible that her mental faculties were impaired; those present certainly thought that she was more than a little distracted and not really aware of what was about to happen to her.

Although she was eventually persuaded to kneel and lay her head on the block, the headsman was young and inexperienced: in fact he had never beheaded anybody before. The reason for this was that the chief executioner for London had been despatched to the north of England to deal with those to be executed in the aftermath of a rebellion known as the Wakefield Plot. The young man who was standing in for him was, according to another witness of Margaret Pole's botched execution, 'a wretched and blundering youth who literally hacked her head and shoulders to pieces in the most pitiful manner'. This apprentice took eleven blows with the axe to remove the woman's head, hacking away at her shoulders and removing the top of her head like a boiled egg in the process. As somebody else present that day remarked, 'he fetched off her head very slovenly'.

The eleven attempts to remove the Countess of Salisbury's head rank as a British record. The ideal was of course to take off the head with one clean blow and this was frequently achieved. It was not uncommon though for two or three or even four or five chops to be required. It was vital that the condemned person should remain perfectly still during this ordeal, so that the whole thing could be accomplished as quickly as could be. Without the assistance and obedience of the condemned person, executions by beheading could easily become very painful for the victim and exceedingly distressing for the onlookers.

Lord William Russell was alleged to have been involved in the Rye House Plot to assassinate Charles II and his brother. At any rate, he was convicted of treason and sentenced to death by beheading. The man appointed to undertake this task was the London hangman, John Ketch. He was more often known as Jack Ketch and under that name became a stock figure in Punch and Judy shows during the nineteenth century. Lord Russell gave Ketch a very generous tip the night before he died, a purse containing ten golden guineas.

The execution of Lord Russell took place in Lincoln's Inn Fields, near the London district of Holborn, on 21 July 1683. Everything went smoothly until the moment that Russell knelt and placed his neck upon the wooden block. He gave no signal to the headsman to indicate when he was ready, something which Jack Ketch later complained of. Whatever the reason, and there was much debate about it later, the first swing of the axe struck Lord Russell not on the neck, but rather the shoulder. Whereupon he twisted his head round and said angrily to the executioner, 'You dog! Did I give you ten guineas to use me so inhumanly?' This irritable criticism from a customer seemed, quite understandably, to put Jack Ketch off his stroke, and his next blow also missed Russell's neck, striking him on the back of the head. It took a further three swipes to remove the head. The diarist John Evelyn, who witnessed the execution, wrote later that it had been done in a, 'butcherly fashion'. There was so much adverse comment on the way that he had handled this job that Ketch took the quite extraordinary step of writing an account of the execution, explaining exactly what had gone wrong, and publishing it as a pamphlet. Called *Apologie by Jack Ketch Esquire*, it advanced a number of ingenious explanations as to why the person to blame for the bungling of the beheading was not the executioner, but rather the victim!

Ketch's account of Lord Russell's execution makes fascinating reading. Its stated purpose was to deal with 'Those grievous Obliquies and Invectives that have been thrown upon me for not Severing my Lord's Head from his Body at one blow'. So, what actually went wrong and why did it take five blows, instead of the more traditional one, to separate Lord Russell's head from his body? There were, according to Ketch, various good reasons for the mishap. For one thing, Russell:

> did not dispose him for receiving of the fatal Stroke in such a posture as was most suitable, for whereas he should have put his hands before his Breast, or else behind him, he spread them out before him, nor would he be persuaded to give any Signal or pull his Cap over his eyes, which might possibly be the Occasion that discovering the Blow, he somewhat heav'd his Body.

The gist of Jack Ketch's complaint was that Lord Russell didn't know what to do with his hands while having his head chopped off and not only that, he didn't tell the executioner when to strike! Then again, somebody distracted Jack Ketch at the crucial moment. He, 'receav'd some Interruption just as I was taking Aim, and going to give the Blow'. All in all, it was everybody else's fault but his.

It is hardly surprising that when the Duke of Monmouth was faced with the prospect of being beheaded by this same bungler a couple of years later, he should have felt a little uneasy. Monmouth was the illegitimate son of Charles II and after his uncle had ascended the throne as James II, the Duke of Monmouth launched an abortive invasion in the west of England, hoping to seize the crown for himself. On 15 July 1685, Monmouth climbed the steps to the scaffold which had been erected on Tower Hill, close to the Tower of London. Determined to make sure that his own execution would go more smoothly than that of Lord Russell, he handed the executioner some money saying, 'Here are six guineas for you. Pray do your business well. Do not serve me as you did my Lord Russell. I have heard that you struck him three or four times.' Turning to the servant who had accompanied him onto the scaffold, the Duke of Monmouth handed him a small leather bag and said, 'Take these remaining guineas and give them to him if he does his job well.'

All this talk about the botched job which he made of his last beheading two years previously, might have made Jack Ketch a little nervous, perhaps. It could not have helped when Monmouth, after having laid his neck on the block, then decided that he wanted to examine the axe and make sure that it was fit for purpose! He lifted his head and said to the executioner, 'Prithee, let me feel the axe.' After running his finger along the edge, he looked dubious and said, 'I fear that it is not sharp enough'. Jack Ketch assure him that it was both sharp and heavy enough.

The first blow of the axe struck the back of Monmouth's head, causing a good deal of blood to begin flowing. It didn't kill him though and he raised himself up and gave the executioner an indignant look. Once he had placed his neck on the block again, there were two more blows, neither of which succeeded in cutting off the duke's head. At this point. Ketch despaired, throwing down his axe crying, 'I cannot do it, my heart fails me!' The sheriff ordered him sternly to get on with the job, whereupon Jack Ketch struck twice more. Even then, the head was not completely severed and he had to use a knife to finish the job.

The crowd was furious to see the handsome and popular young nobleman being tortured in this way and there were shouts of 'Fling him over the rails!', meaning that they wished the executioner to be given to them. The hostility of the spectators had become so great, that there seemed to be a very real danger of some harm befalling Jack Ketch. As a contemporary source says: 'The crowd was wrought up to such an ecstasy of rage that the executioner was in danger of being torn in pieces, and was conveyed away under a strong guard.'

The trend for making public executions painful, gory or protracted faded away in Britain by the end of the seventeenth century. Not that there were any fewer executions, but those who were put to death in the future were simply disposed of as swiftly and humanely as could be accomplished. Part of this was due to the spirit of the times. The eighteenth century saw the dawn of the Enlightenment, sometimes known as the Age of Reason, and it was felt that the exhibition of men and women being done to death in ingenious ways did not quite fit in with this new age. There was still the occasional mutilation of criminals, but this was invariably done post-mortem. The penalty of hanging, drawing and quartering remained on the statute books until 1870, when it was removed by the Forfeiture Act. Incredibly, beheading was not abolished in Britain until as late as 1973! That was the year that Section 2 of the 1814 Treason Act was repealed by the Statute Law (Repeals) Act 1973. There had not been any beheading of a live person since the execution of Lord Lovatt in 1747, although a few heads had been publicly removed after the death of their owners. The last such occasion was the execution of the Cato Street conspirators in 1820, when five men were hanged and their heads removed after they were dead.

Hanging and firing squads, the only means of capital punishment used in Britain since the middle of the eighteenth century are both unpleasant, but neither really falls into the category of being tortured to death and so the execution of the Duke of Monmouth in 1685 was the last occasion that any execution can be said to have entailed torture.

Chapter 6

Eighteenth and Nineteenth-Century Britain

With the ending of the *Peine Forte et Dure* in 1772, the torture of unconvicted criminals came to a halt in Britain. The use of torture as a punishment, though, continued unabated. One way in which those guilty of certain offences were tortured was by condemning them to stand in the pillory. The pillory is a framework through which a man or woman's head and hands are placed, while the person is standing. The aim is to make them objects of public ridicule, but the reality was that sometimes this ended in prolonged suffering, severe injury or even death. Somebody with their head sticking out of a hole and with their hands restrained from protecting themselves is really very vulnerable. In addition to catcalls and jeers, the crowd of spectators sometimes hurled not only abuse, but also rotten vegetables, refuse from the streets, dead cats, stones and even broken bottles. Being pilloried could, on occasion, be tantamount to a sentence of stoning to death, a most painful way to die. We may see somebody suffering in this way in Illustration 17.

Elizabeth Needham, known popularly as 'Mother Needhamby' ran an exclusive brothel in eighteenth-century London. Most brothels were staffed with experienced prostitutes, but Needham catered for what we might call a niche market, those men who wished to have sex with very young virgins. There was incidentally at that time a widespread belief that having sexual intercourse with a virgin would cure venereal diseases such as syphilis. Elizabeth Needham fulfilled the needs of such men by recruiting young girls, fresh from the country, who had come to the capital to seek their fortune. She did not at first reveal her true occupation, but managed to trick many girls into working at her brothel. Needham was a well-known figure in London during the 1720s, being immortalized, improbably enough, in both engravings and poetry. Hogarth used her as the model for 'Moll Hackabout' in his series of engravings, 'The Harlot's Progress', while she also featured in Alexander Pope's satire, *The Dunciad*.

All good things come to an end and in 1731 an attempt was made to clean up London a little by cracking down on prostitution and closing down brothels. Despite the fact that her establishment was patronised by the aristocracy, as well as many high-ranking army officers, Mother Needham's house was raided and she was arrested. On 29 April 1731, she as convicted of keeping a disorderly house and fined a shilling (5p). This was a remarkably lenient punishment, but Needham was also sentenced to stand twice in the pillory and it was this prospect which was terrifying to the woman. Needham had been a familiar enough character to the upper echelons of society, who were prepared to tolerate the sexual exploitation of innocent young lasses from the provinces, but the London mob was another matter entirely. News of Elizabeth Needham's activities had, following her appearance in court, spread far and wide and great disgust was felt among ordinary working-class Londoners, for somebody who could lure girls into such a trap.

The authorities knew that Needham would face a rough time when she stood in the pillory and so an unprecedented step was taken. The chief danger for an unpopular person in the pillory was injuries to the head and face. People had been blinded by things hurled at their faces with great violence and others had died. Elizabeth Needham, it was decided, need not actually stand in the pillory, but could lie on the scaffold in front of it. This, it was thought, would protect her from some of the worst of the crowd's anger. It was a vain hope.

On 2 May, Mother Needham appeared on the scaffold and lay down in front of the pillory. For an hour, she was bombarded with stones, rocks and bricks and was carried back to prison in a lamentable state. She expressed hysterical terror at the prospect of her second public exposure, which was due to take place two days later, but she needn't have worried. The following day, 3 May, she died of her injuries.

Deaths by stoning were not especially common in Britain in the eighteenth century, but nor were they very rare. The year after Elizabeth Needham's death, somebody else was killed in the pillory. John Waller hit upon a very easy way of making money. In the early eighteenth century, the authorities were very keen to stamp out highway robbery and other forms of theft. One way of doing this was to offer large cash rewards to those who informed on criminals, the money only being payable on the conviction of those arrested. John Waller formed a gang and together they accused complete strangers of capital offences, arranging for groups of witnesses to give false testimony in order to obtain convictions. In this way, a number of wholly innocent men were convicted of capital crimes.

As is so often the way when some ingenious moneymaking scheme is devised, Waller and his cronies eventually went too far and he found himself being arrested and charged with perjury. He was fined and given a prison term, but before serving that, was to be set in the pillory for an hour at Seven Dials, at that time one of the roughest parts of London. John Waller didn't last an hour in the pillory. He was stoned and beaten to death within a short time. At the subsequent inquest, the jury brought in a verdict of, 'wilful murder by persons unknown'. A contemporary report describes in detail what happened to Waller:

> Last Tuesday John Waller was brought to Seven Dyals, in the parish of St.
> Giles's in the Fields, to stand in the pillory (for the first time) according

to the Sentence passed on him last session, for swearing against several innocent persons of robbing him on the Highway in different counties, by which they were convicted and near being executed. After he had stood upon the pillory for about three minutes, in which time he was most furiously pelted with large stones, pieces of bottle and colliflower stalks, by which he was very much cut in his face and head: then a Chimney Sweeper jumped up to him and pulled him down from the pillory, and tore all his cloaths off leaving only his stockings and shoes on. After that they beat him and kicked him and jumped upon him as he lay on the ground till they killed him. On Wednesday evening the Coroner's inquest sat on the body and brought in their verdict Wilful Murder, with unlawful weapons.

In 1753, a group of men came up with an enterprise which was similar in some ways to that for which John Waller ultimately paid with his life. They told a poor man called Tyler that they had no further use for the horse belonging to one of them and made a gift of it to him. Surprised, but pleased, Tyler rode off down the road, only to find himself being detained a few minutes by another member of the gang, who claimed that the horse was his and that Tyler must have stolen it. Others in the group gave supporting evidence, with the result that Tyler was hanged for horse theft. The gang split the reward between themselves and then inevitably, began pulling the same trick on a regular basis until they were caught. All four were sentenced to seven years imprisonment for perjury, but were first to spend an hour in the pillory. The story of what happened next is told by *The Newgate Chronicle*:

> March 5th, 1756, M'Daniel and Berry were set on the pillory at the end of Hatton Garden, and were so severely treated by the populace that their lives were supposed to be in danger.
>
> Egan and Salmon were taken to Smithfield on Monday the eighth of the same month, amidst a surprising concourse of people, who no sooner saw the offenders exposed on the pillory, than they pelted them with stones, brick-bats, potatoes, dead dogs and cats, and other things. The constables now interposed; but being soon overpowered, the offenders were left wholly to the mercy of an enraged mob. The blows they received occasioned their heads to swell to an enormous size; and they were nearly strangled by people hanging to the skirts of their coats. They had been on the pillory about half an hour, when a stone striking Egan on the head, he immediately expired.

It is reasonable to include in a book devoted to judicial torture the incidents of stoning to death by crowds cited above. Those who ordered these people to be publicly exhibited could have been in no doubt about the reaction of the mob when presented with these helpless victims. Just as in the authorized and legally-mandated deaths by stoning which are a feature of certain Middle Eastern counties like Iran, the pillorying of people in eighteenth-century Britain was a deliberate decision by the courts to allow the population to express their detestation of particular offences. Elizabeth Needham's death could have come as no surprise to anybody. It is this, the calculated exposure of individuals convicted by the courts to injury and pain, which made the pillory, in many cases, an instrument of judicial torture. Punishment in the pillory lingered on into the nineteenth century, although becoming increasingly uncommon. In 1816, it was abolished for all offences other than perjury and then, a little over twenty years later in 1837, it was entirely done away with.

The public exhibition of those guilty of breaking the law was not limited to being held in the pillory. For many years, two ways of punishing those of whom society disapproved by subjecting them to humiliation and pain were used exclusively on women. The first of these was the cucking or ducking stool and although it has come to be seen as a fairly trivial and relatively harmless punishment, a little thought will show that it was anything but and certainly deserves to be treated as an instrument of torture.

The ordeal of cold water, at which we have looked in previous chapters, was a means to see whom the baptismal water would reject. Suspected criminals, especially witches, were thrown into a pond or lake and if they floated, were then adjudged guilty. This method of determining innocence or guilt was revived in the mid-seventeenth century by Matthew Hopkins, the self-styled 'Witchfinder General'. At about the same time that immersion in cold water was falling into disuse as a means of establishing guilt, it began to grow in popularity as a punishment in its own right.

During the Middle Ages, there was a tradition of exposing minor offenders to public ridicule by setting them in a 'cucking chair', just as some people were set in the pillory or stocks. The etymology of the cucking stool is a curious one. It derives its name from an Old English verb 'cukken', which means to defecate. A literal translation of 'cucking stool', the earliest mention of which dates from the thirteenth century, might perhaps be 'Shitting Chair'!

Originally, the cucking stool was a static feature and the offender, a scolding woman or dishonest tradesman for example, was secured to it and the public were able to express their contempt. This was harmless enough. In time, wheels were added to some of these chairs and they were drawn around the village or town, accompanied by a jeering crowd. Sometime in the sixteenth century, a further refinement was added to the cucking stool. Although it had begun as a mild way for ordinary people to express their feelings about bakers who adulterated their flour or women who behaved in scandalous ways, by the end of the sixteenth century, the cucking stool was reserved only for women. It was at this time, in 1597, that the term 'ducking stool' first appeared.

Because only a single letter distinguishes the cucking stool from the ducking stool, it is sometimes claimed that one is merely a corruption of the other, but this is quite untrue. Although the name of cucking stool continued to be used alongside that of ducking stool, the two things were entirely separate and distinct. The purpose of the ducking stool was not only to expose a woman, chiefly those found guilty of scolding or gossiping, to ridicule, but also to make them suffer a little physically.

The most common type of ducking stool was made in the following way. A wooden trolley had attached to it a long beam, something like a see-saw. At one end of this beam was a chair, in which a woman could be strapped. Once this had been done, the device was pushed along, usually with a rowdy crowd accompanying it, until the village pond or other convenient body of water was reached. Then the chair was manoeuvred until it was above the water and the beam lowered, so that the woman was submerged. Such a procedure may be seen in Illustration 18. Another version was a bit like a tumbril, with the chair being at the end of two shafts, like those from a cart. This was backed into the water, with the same result, that the victim would be completely submerged beneath the surface. In some places, there were also fixed ducking stools, which were attached to stout posts which were driven into the bank of a pond or river.

On the face of it, dipping somebody in a smelly pond sounds more like a harmless prank than anything. However, women actually died in the ducking stool, while others suffered terribly. In the first place, imagine being secured in a chair, entirely at the mercy of others, who lowered you beneath the water. Inevitably, some of those carrying out this activity would leave the victim under water for longer than others. It was meant to be a swift dip, but in some cases, the woman, who might be quite elderly, was left for a while. Then too, accidents happened, when people lost their grip on the other end of the beam and it took time to regain control of the thing. Imagine being held under water in that way, even for ten or twenty seconds. It could be a terrifying ordeal.

There was an even greater danger than the risk of accidental drowning and that was that the shock of sudden immersion in cold water could actually cause a person's heart to stop beating. This well-known physiological reaction is called Cold Shock Response or Sudden Immersion Syndrome. It is what most commonly kills people who fall through thin ice, rather than their drowning. Some women being ducked died as soon as they went under the water. The older or feebler a person, the more likely is this to happen. What looks like a bit of malicious pleasure in the humiliation of a woman turns into an impromptu execution.

The same thing had been observed in the Middle Ages, when those subjected to the ordeal of cold water also died when they were thrown into the pond or lake. Even under ideal circumstances, when those operating the ducking stool were not too ill-disposed towards the person whom they were punishing, being ducked in this way could be a traumatic experience. Few of us would like to face the prospect of being half-drowned in this way.

The heyday of the ducking stool was the late seventeenth century, when many towns and villages had their own ducking stools which could be used against prostitutes, scolds and other troublesome women. Some explanation of what is meant by the expression, 'scold' might be helpful at this point. A 'common scold' was a legal term to describe a woman who habitually breached the peace by quarrelling with her neighbours or abusing her husband so that others could hear the disturbance. The Latin term for the common scold, *communis rixatrix*, makes it clear that only a woman could be guilty of this offence. The clue is in the 'ix' ending to the noun. We still see this used occasionally to distinguish males from females. In the 1930s, male pilots such as Charles Lindbergh were sometimes described as 'aviators'. When a woman such as Amy Johnson or Amelia Earheart became famous, she was invariably called an 'aviatrix' instead. And of course the expression 'dominatrix', for a female dominator, is current to this day!

In the late eighteenth century Sir William Blackstone, the famous jurist, gave a description of both the offence of being a common scold and also its punishment. Writing in his *Commentaries on the Laws of England*, he said:

> Lastly, a common scold, communis rixatrix, (for our law-latin confines it to the feminine gender) is a public nuisance to her neighbourhood. For which offence she may be indicted; and, if convicted, shall be sentenced to be placed in a certain engine of correction called the trebucket, castigatory, or cucking stool, which in the Saxon language signifies the scolding stool; though now it is frequently corrupted into ducking stool, because the residue of the judgment is, that, when she is so placed therein, she shall be plunged in the water for her punishment.

A typical sentence from the magistrates in the Yorkshire town of Wakefield in 1671 reads as follows:

> Foresasmuch as Jane, wife of William Farrett, shoemaker, stands indicted for a common scold, to the great annoyance and disturbance of her neighbours. It is therefore ordered that she should be openly ducked, and ducked over the head and ears by the constables of Selby, for which this call be their warrant.

The great advantage of the ducking stool was that it could be administered swiftly and the cost was minimal. Once the machine itself was made, it would last forever. There is to this day an eighteenth-century ducking stool on display in the parish church of Leominster and it is in such good condition that it looks as though it would still serve its original purpose. Of course, having constructed the ducking stool, it was wise to ensure that there was a deep-enough body of water to use it. There are records of women being taken to the river or pond, only for the crowd to be disappointed because the level was too low to submerge anybody. The parish records of Southam in Warwickshire from 1718 contain a bill for 9s 6d which was paid to have the village pond dredged, so that it would be deep enough for the ducking stool to be used.

A typical example of how the ducking stool operated, and for what offences, may be seen in the town of Kingston, nowadays virtually a suburb of London, but in the eighteenth century a small town on the bank of the river Thames. In April 1745, the landlord of the Queen's Head grew so tired of being nagged by his wife that he applied to the local magistrates to put a stop to it. The magistrates ordered that his wife should be ducked in the Thames. This was duly done on 27 April 1745, before a crowd numbering around 3,000.

The records for the Kingston ducking stool are still around and give us some insight into the expense to a parish of acquiring one of these devices. In the Churchwardens and Chamberlain's accounts for the district in 1672, we see a bill for £1 3s 4d for constructing the ducking stool, which is roughly £1.17p in today's prices. Over the years, there are various small costs for repairing and maintaining it.

Although no law was ever passed forbidding its use, the ducking stool, like the pillory and stocks, became less popular towards the end of the eighteenth century and there are only one or two cases of its use in the early nineteenth century. In 1808, a Mrs Ganble was ducked in Plymouth and the following year, Jenny Pipes was ducked at Leominster, using the same machine which can be seen to this day in the church there. Eight years later, an attempt was made to duck Sarah Leeke, but the water level in the pond was found to be too low and she was instead paraded around the town in the ducking stool. This is the last recorded use of the ducking stool in Britain.

Curiously enough, although the use of the ducking stool fell into disuse, the offence of being a common scold lingered on until well into the twentieth century! Although prosecutions were unknown for over a century, it was not until the passing of the Criminal Law Act in 1967 that common scolds were relegated to the history books.

Ducking stools were an English custom which crossed the Atlantic with the Puritans in the seventeenth century and were in use even later than in Britain.

There are a number of accounts of troublesome women being ducked for nagging their husbands or arguing too vociferously with their neighbours. The last recorded ducking in America was of Mary Davis in 1819.

One last means of causing pain which was used only on women was the scold's bridle, also known in Scotland as the branks. This was an open metal framework which was fastened around the woman's head. A piece of metal protruded into the mouth and prevented her from speaking. This sounds harmless enough, except that in practice these things could cause great pain and severe injury. The scold's bridle was used for much the same reasons as the ducking stool, that is to say for quarrelsome or aggressive women who were in the habit of creating a disturbance. The idea was to curb their tongues and stop them from using their voices for a while. Sometimes, particularly in Scotland, there was a more sinister purpose for the scold's bridle. It was known there not only as the branks, but also as the 'witch's bridle'. The idea behind it was that when being imprisoned or tortured, a witch might be able to say a spell which would either allow her to escape or alternatively protect her from pain. Silencing her with a sharp piece of metal over her tongue would prevent this.

The usual time in the scold's bridle would only be for an hour or two, during which time the 'scold' might typically be chained in a public place. Just as with the ducking stool, part of the punishment was being exposed to public mockery. There was more to it than that though, as George Riley Scott explains in his classic work, *A History of Torture*, first published in 1940;

> The bridle was constructed of iron, something after the fashion of a helmet, except that it was merely a framework, and offered no obstruction to the sight, or the movement of anything other than the tongue, which projected into the mouth, acting as a gag; and, it may be stated, an exceedingly uncomfortable and cruel gag at that.

In fact, many women suffered lacerations to their tongues and the inside of their mouths, the severity of which depended upon the construction of the gag part of the bridle. In some examples, the gag is simply a smooth and flat piece of iron, but in others it is covered in sharp spikes, so that even moving the head from side to side could cause cuts to the roof of the mouth. Even an hour in such a contraption would certain constitute torture and we must remember that in Scotland such things were left on suspected witches for days at a time. George Riley Scott again;

> The specimens which have been preserved in many museums throughout the kingdom indicate the variety of designs that were used, some of which were undoubtedly capable of inflicting severe pain and injury, and the

wearing of which, even for a short time, must have constituted a form of torture. In some cases the part which penetrated the mouth was sharply rowelled like a spur, or studded with spikes.

Sometimes when thinking of torture, we become sidetracked by considering specific manifestations of the phenomenon such as the rack in the Tower of London. This can distract us from the essential nature of the act itself and means sometimes that we don't recognize acts of torture when we see them. Recollecting now the definition at which we looked in the introduction to this book, torture is the inflicting of severe pain, either as punishment or to make people do or say something. Working by this idea of torture, there can be no doubt that flogging is a type of torture. After all, the whole aim of judicial flogging or whipping is to cause severe pain! Otherwise, it would be a pointless exercise.

Before looking at the use of flogging in the eighteenth and nineteenth centuries, it is worth remembering that this form of torture was still going strong in the British Isles until well within living memory. The last use of the birch, as ordered by a court in the Isle of Man, was as recent as 1976. The cat-o'-nine-tails was still being used in England in 1962 and its use didn't officially end for another five years. By then, of course, the practice had been greatly modified and restricted, with various safeguards and limitations built in to prevent serious harm. Flogging with the cat-o'-nine-tails was still technically torture, of course, but increasingly rare as the twentieth century progressed.

It might help to see whipping for what it really was, which is to say a torture of varying degrees of severity, if we look at a specific example of how it was carried out in practice. During the reign of Charles II a crank Protestant clergyman called Titus Oates came up with the idea that there was a plot against the king's life, which was orchestrated by the Catholics. This played to some of the deepest anxieties of the age and the Popish Plot, as it became known, turned into a hysterical witch hunt for Jesuit conspirators. The truth was that Oates had invented the whole thing and this became generally known, although not until fifteen people, including the Archbishop of Armagh, had been executed on his perjured evidence.

There is of course a modern saying, to the effect that what goes around, comes around, and the accession of Charles II's brother James in 1685 was a neat illustration of this mechanism. James was of course a Catholic and as soon as he was on the throne, he saw to it that Titus Oates was arrested, charged with perjury and brought before the notorious Judge Jeffreys, who was now Lord Chancellor. After being convicted, a sentence was passed on Oates which was widely thought to be an attempt to have him done to death without the formality of a death sentence. The problem was that perjury was a misdemeanour at law and not a felony. This meant that it was not possible to hang somebody for the offence. However, the next best thing was decreed. He was to be set in the pillory and then whipped at the cart's tail from Aldgate to Newgate. Then, forty-eight hours later, he was to be whipped from Newgate to Tyburn and then imprisoned for life. The words of the sentence set out clearly and explicitly what the wretched man might expect:

> First, The Court does order for a fine, that you pay 1000 marks upon each Indictment. Secondly, That you be stript of all your Canonical Habits. Thirdly, the Court does award, That you do stand upon the Pillory, and in the Pillory, here before Westminster-hall gate, upon Monday next, for an hour's time, between the hours of 10 and 12; with a paper over your head (which you must first walk with round about to all the Courts in Westminister-hall) declaring your crime. And that is upon the first Indictment.Fourthly, (on the Second Indictment), upon Tuesday, you shall stand upon, and in the Pillory, at the Royal Exchange in London, for the space of an hour, between the hours of twelve and two; with the same inscription. You shall upon the next Wednesday be whipped from Aldgate to Newgate. Upon Friday, you shall be whipped from Newgate to Tyburn, by the hands of the common hangman.

Few thought that the one-time vicar would survive this terrible punishment.

It should be explained that when whipping somebody, the extent of the injury and pain can be varied tremendously. A whip can be wielded so that it leaves merely a reddened patch of skin, causes a bruise or actually breaks the skin and allows blood to flow. In the case of Titus Oates, it was strongly suspected that the hangman, who administered the punishment, had been given special instructions not to spare his victim.

On the day of the first whipping, Oates was brought from his cell and stripped to the waist. Then his hands were tied together and lashed to the back of a cart. The cart then set off towards Newgate Prison, a distance by road of about a mile and a half. It was not long before the prisoner's back was a mass of bloody welts and there was some speculation among those observing the event that he might be dead before he even reached Newgate. However, he survived, although by the end of the journey he was no longer able to walk and was simply being dragged through the mud, semi-conscious, while the hangman still lashed him.

The following day, it was clear that Oates was in a pitiful condition and it seemed that he might not be able to survive another flogging. Representations were made to James II, to see if there was any chance that he would extend mercy and say that the flogging due on Friday, which was to be from Newgate Prison to Tyburn, the site of present-day Marble Arch, might be either postponed or perhaps remitted entirely. The king was having none of it. He said bluntly, 'He shall go though it if he has breath in his body!' The following day, Titus Oates was unable to walk and so was tied to a sled and dragged along what is now Oxford Street, with the hangman lashing him all the way. Somebody who dressed Oates' wounds counted no fewer than 1,700 stripes, perhaps a record. Nevertheless, Oates survived the savage flogging which he received and spent the next three years in prison, being finally released when James II was overthrown and replaced by the staunchly Protestant William and Mary in 1688.

There was an enormous variation in how whippings were carried out during the seventeenth and eighteenth centuries. Sometimes, an ordinary cartwhip would be used, on others a length of rope. The severity of the thing also varied a great deal. At times, as with Titus Oates, the victim would be left half dead by the experience. Sometimes, though, the flogging was almost symbolic and the main object of the exercise was to display the person publicly; this humiliation was felt to be very great in itself. We are used today to the sight of any amount of bare flesh, but in the eighteenth century, it was all but unheard-of for people to strip to the waist publicly. When being whipped though, both men and women might have to remove their clothes in this way. This, at least as much as the actual whipping, would be a punishment.

Flogging in prisons, used to control violent or dangerous prisoners, was used throughout the nineteenth century, but whipping as a judicial punishment gradually faded away. It was of course still on the statute book for things such as vagrancy and slaughtering animals without a licence, but the Victorians seemed to sense that tying men up and whipping them like animals did not really accord with the image which they had of themselves as being a civilized society. It was this, as much as anything else, which brought about the end of public executions in 1868. The carnival atmosphere and ribald carryings-on that accompanied public hangings were felt to belong to a cruder and less sophisticated age. That sort of thing might have been all right for the Georgians, but times had changed. It was much the same with the whipping post. Its time had passed. Then, in the 1860s, something happened which altered all this and brought about the return of flogging as something which the courts might impose.

The passing of the Security of the Persons of Her Majesty's Subjects from Personal Violence Act 1863 signalled a new and hardening attitude on the part of both the legislature and judiciary to violent crime and an attempt to counter one sort of violence with another. In short, those who hurt people would in turn have pain inflicted upon them to discourage them from acting so in the future. The act, which provided for flogging with the cat-o'-nine-tails as a penalty for robbery with violence, was introduced to combat a wave of muggings which swept through the larger cities of England in the 1850s. The muggers were known as 'garrotters', because they typically worked in pairs, one grabbing the victim around his throat and choking him, while as accomplice rifled through the pockets of the helpless person.

The activities of the garrotters turned into what is sometimes known as a 'moral panic', when society becomes persuaded that some dreadful evil is befalling it and that a certain type crime or particular sort of person needs to be tackled. Transportation to Australia was coming to an end and some criminals were being released from prison after completing just part of their sentence, a common practice today, but in the 1850s a new and dangerous experiment. The idea took hold that it was these 'ticket-of-leave men', who had been given remission on their sentences, who were chiefly responsible for the outbreak of violence on the streets. Something needed to be done, but nobody could think what, other than the obvious expedient of increasing the length of the prison sentences given to such people when caught. Some were given twenty years and others life, with hard labour. The street robberies continued.

In the early hours of Wednesday, 16 July 1862, Hugh Pilkington, Liberal MP for Blackburn, was walking home from a late sitting of the Commons. As he passed the Reform Club in Pall Mall, two men rushed him, knocking him to the ground. As he lay there, stunned, his watch was snatched and the two robbers sprinted off into the darkness. Pilkington had not been mugged in some dark alleyway in a seedy part of a provincial town. This was one of the grandest streets in the heart of the capital, a few hundred yards from Buckingham Palace. Seeing one of their own fall prey to the crime wave galvanized Parliament into action. The response was the Security of the Persons of her Majesty's Subjects from Personal Violence Act, more commonly known as the Garrotters' Act. Before the passing of this act, muggers had usually been prosecuted under Section 43 of the Larceny Act, which provided for a maximum sentence of hard labour for life for anybody convicted of robbery with violence. The new act was punishable with both lengthy prison sentences, but in addition, up to fifty strokes with the 'cat'. The cat-o'-nine-tails had been used for years in the British army and navy. It consisted of a wooden handle, which was 19in long, attached to which were nine cords, each 33in long. It was applied to the bare back of the person being punished and caused a tremendous amount of pain.

During the nineteenth century, newspaper reporters were allowed into prisons to witness both executions and floggings. For this reason, there are a number of vivid descriptions of just what 'garrotters' faced when they were caught. On 17 January 1867, two men who had been convicted under the Garrotters' Act each received two dozen strokes of the 'cat' before being locked up for many years. The scene in York Prison was a grim one:

> The prisoner was fastened to the triangle by straps at ankles, knees and hands and a leather band was placed around the neck to prevent the

lash hitting the victim in that part of the body. The 'operators' upon the occasion were two warders of the gaol, who administered in each instance a dozen strokes in succession.

The first descent of the whip made him cry 'Oh,' in a piteous tone, and at the second he cried out 'Oh dear,' after the forth he begged for and was given a glass of water; and at the ninth he resisted so strongly, though without the least avail, that the framework to which he was bound was moved slightly from its original starting point. As the blows followed each other in quick succession his cries of suffering were louder and more frequent. It was in vain that he asked for mercy or, in a dreadful paroxysm of pain, promised that he would 'never do so again'.

After the twenty-fout lashes had been given to the two men, they were allowed to return to their cells. Illustration 19 shows the scene after a prisoner has been flogged in this way.

It has to be said that the 'cat' made little difference to the prevalence of mugging in the cities of Victorian Britain. It is not savage punishments which deter crime, but rather the likelihood of being caught. Since the chances of getting away with such robberies were good, the actual penalty for those arrested and convicted was an irrelevance to the average violent criminal.

Throughout most of the nineteenth century, many prisoners in in British prisons were routinely and regularly tortured by means of devices which had been specially designed to break their spirits and subdue their bodies. No account of torture during those years would be complete without a description of the treadmill and crank, machines built with no other aim than to cause suffering and exhaustion. Some readers might vaguely have heard of the treadmill; few will be aware of the crank, the treadmill's smaller relative. The story of their origins is an interesting one.

William Cubitt was an eminent civil engineer in Victorian Britain, later to be knighted for his work on a variety of projects, including railways and waterworks. He was also a millwright, specializing in the construction of windmills, a fact which may have had some bearing on his most famous invention. In 1816, the 31-year-old engineer visited Bury St Edmunds Prison and noted that the prisoners there were doing nothing but lounge about the yard. This seemed to him to be an unhealthy state of affairs. He was visiting the prison with a magistrate, who said to him, 'I wish to God, Mr Cubitt, you could suggest to us some mode of employing these fellows.' Cubitt's own recollection was that he replied, 'Something has struck me which may prove worthy of further consideration, and perhaps you will hear from me upon the subject.' Whether, even during the Regency period, men really did hold conversations in such a stilted and measured fashion is an interesting point! At any rate, within a couple of months William Cubitt had come up with an ingenious, if cruel, idea. What he thought might keep all those prisoners busy was if they were to be set to work climbing what was, to all intents and purposes, an endless staircase. And so the treadmill was born, the first being built at Brixton prison in 1817.

The treadmill is rather like a very elongated waterwheel. Those walking on it are separated from each other by wooden partitions and face a blank wall. While holding onto the rail in front of them, they are obliged to step upwards constantly, so turning the wheel. The usual pattern was that each man would spend fifteen minutes on the treadmill and then rest for five before resuming the activity. The amount of energy expended on this task was enormous. It varied from prison to prison, but at Brixton, Reading and Guildford, each man was required to climb the equivalent of 13,000ft a day. This is like climbing to the top of Ben Nevis, Britain's highest mountain, three times, every day, day in and day out!

Few men, even the fittest and most athletic, were capable of maintaining this level of effort for long, especially on the restricted prison diet, and the result was that even the most aggressive and refractory convicts were left exhausted and unable to find the strength to do anything much at the end of the day. The treadmill certainly kept them fully occupied and ensured that they had no energy for fighting or rioting, which was, after all, the object of the exercise. So effective was the treadmill at subduing unruly prisoners and leaving them like lifeless automata by the evening that many prisons adopted them. They were the ideal way of ensuring that those sentenced to 'hard labour' actually spent their days in a gruelling and exhausting way. There was another aspect of the treadmill which made it even more soul-destroying and that was the utter futility of the thing. It is quite likely that when William Cubitt first dreamed up the treadmill, he based it upon the waterwheel, which is generally used for turning millstones to grind wheat into flour. After all, as well as being an engineer, Cubitt was also a millwright. Experiments were made with using the rotating axle of the treadmill for grinding flour, at Bedford prison for instance, but the idea never really caught on. It was easier just to let the machine grind on pointlessly, rather than add additional parts which would all need to be serviced and maintained. It was this pointlessness which caused the treadmill to be widely loathed by the prisoners. They came up with various slang terms for the thing, all of which tended to refer to the aimless nature of the task. They called a spell on the treadmill, 'grinding the wind' and the machine itself, 'the everlasting staircase'. The expression, 'grinding the wind' was a reference to the fact that at some prisons, the treadmill was linked up to a windmill, in order to slow down the pace a little. Men would spend the daylight hours labouring away, with no other result than to turn the sails of the windmill above their heads.

The staff in prisons were very keen on the new method for keeping their charges occupied and out of mischief. Within a few years of the first treadmill being set up at Brixton, prisons across the whole of Britain had them installed. Here is an account by the chaplain of Bedford prison in 1822 of what he saw as the beneficial effects on the men:

> Whether it be the means of repressing crime, and inducing habits of industry among those who are now wearied with its labour, we have not yet had experience enough to determine. All that can be said at present is, that for a time it subdues the mind and fatigues the body without at all affecting the general health of the prisoners or in any way injuring their frame. In the last Quarter, as well as in the preceding one, there has been a greater number of prisoners in custody than was ever known in this County at this season of the year and some of these have been men whose habits and general characters are of the worst description. With the present means of employment however, it has not been found difficult to govern them, and they have all been for the most part submissive and peaceable; tho; I fear, little hope can be entertained of their effectual reformation.

There was one great disadvantage to the treadmill from the point of view of the prison authorities. This was that it required supervision and active participation by the staff. A whistle had to be blown every fifteen minutes, to signal the change of shift, the men had to be watched, to ensure that they did not attempt to talk to each other and when, as sometimes happened, a man refused to continue, it would be necessary to take him off to the punishment cells. There was also the feeling that having a large number of prisoners congregating together in one place at the same time, was a bad thing in itself. The chaplain at Preston prison in 1826 was particularly worried about this feature of the treadmill:

> The tread mill has been constantly at work during the last twelve months, and it still continues to be a source of great terror and a means of severe punishment. It would be improper, however, in the chaplain to conceal that he is disappointed, with regard to many of the prisoners, in the moral effect which he had anticipated from its use. The benefit which might arise from the punishment is counteracted by the disadvantages always attendant upon bringing together a great number of prisoners.

All these difficulties were neatly obviated by the successor to the treadmill, which was the crank. The crank was a large iron drum, sometimes enclosed within a wooden box. Inside, was sand or gravel and a number of scoops, mounted on a wheel. This could be turned by a handle protruding from the drum. It took a considerable amount of effort to turn this handle, which had to be done with both hands and the man bending his body and exerting himself quite hard. A typical resistance was set at 12lbs. As the wheel inside turned, the scoops picked up sand and then emptied it back again when they reached the top of the cycle. That was all there was to this fiendishly simple but very debilitating machine. One last detail was that a dial fixed to the front of the machine counted the number of revolutions. It was the ultimate in pointless occupation and there was no pretence at all that the crank was meant to be other than a punishment, the 'hard labour' part of a sentence of imprisonment.

The crank was installed in the prisoner's cell and there was consequently no need for anybody to supervise its use. A glance at the dial could tell an officer immediately how much labour had been undertaken. It was necessary for each man or boy, for the crank was given to children as well, to turn the handle 10,000 times each day. If the required number of revolutions were not completed, then there would be no meal. To earn breakfast, 2,000 turns had to be accomplished. Then another 3,000 had to be done before lunch and 3,000 again before the evening meal. The remaining 2,000 turns had to be done before the prisoner could sleep.

It was estimated that to turn the handle of the crank 10,000 times meant expending roughly a quarter of the work that a draught-horse would carry out in a day. This was enormously taxing for an adult man, but for boys it was often beyond the limit of their endurance. Young people could be and were driven to suicide by the demands made upon them. A healthy boy might be able to perform perhaps a tenth of the work of a draught-horse, demanding two or three times this amount of work, especially on the meagre diet in a prison would lead eventually to starvation and wasting away.

The reasons for the popularity of the crank with prison authorities was twofold. On the one hand, no officers were needed to supervise the activity. With the treadmill, a squad of warders had to keep a constant watch on the activity, to ensure that nobody was talking and that no fights broke out. With cellular labour on the crank, nothing of the sort was necessary. The door was locked and the prisoner knew that if he didn't get on and complete the task, then he would be eating nothing but bread and having nothing but water to drink. Instead of being guarded and controlled, the onus was on the prisoner to get on with the task.

The second great advantage with the crank was the sheer and utter futility of the exercise. In some prisons, Chelmsford for instance, the treadmill was operating an actual mill which produced flour. The men walking up what they termed the 'endless staircase' knew that their work was accomplishing something. This might have lessened the grinding monotony of the thing and given them a sense of purpose. Not so with the crank! They knew that their work turning the handle of the dreaded machine was completely pointless, just scooping up sand and dropping it again. The idea of labouring like a beast of burden, day in and day out in this fashion, is a horrifying one. This was the whole idea, that it not only exhausted a man physically, but also crushed his spirit at the same time.

There was something quintessentially Victorian about compelling men and boys to slave away for the good of their souls like this, performing pointless work on the treadmill and crank. As the Victorian Age drew to a close though, more enlightened minds in the field of penology saw what a terrible business it was to break men in this way. Although by the 1870s most English prisons had installed treadmills, their days were numbered. The popularity of the treadmill in the 1870s was a direct result of a law which was passed in 1865. The Prison Act laid it down as a legal requirement that any male over the age of 16 who had been sentenced to hard labour had to spend at least three months of the sentence undertaking labour of the first class, which meant the treadmill or crank.

Times were changing by the 1890s and in 1894 the Departmental Commission on Prisons was established, under the chairmanship of Herbert Gladstone. When this committee issued its report the following year, it made a number of what seemed at the time to be radical recommendations. For one thing, the committee concluded that the best way of reducing crime was to improve the lot of the average working man, a conclusion which must have sounded dangerously like socialism to many respectable Victorians! It was also strongly suggested that the treadmill and crank be abolished. In 1895, the year that the Gladstone Commission published its report, there were thirty-nine treadmills in English prisons and twenty-nine cranks. It was to take time to change the law, but the report's recommendations were acted upon in some prisons immediately. Within five years all but thirteen treadmills and five cranks had been dismantled. The 1898 Prison Act sounded the death-knell for the treadmill and crank. Along with another of the Gladstone Commission's recommendations, that boys and men were to be separated in prisons, this act changed the British penal system beyond all recognition. The last treadmill in England ceased operation in 1901.

So far, we have been looking at punishments which have been carried out in accordance with civil law, the ordinary law of the land. Matters were a little different in the armed forces, not least because the standards of evidence to convict a man were often lower during a court martial than in a civil court. Another point to consider is that punishments of varying severity, some of them sufficient to cause extreme pain and even death, could be carried out in the army and navy without the necessity for any formal legal proceedings. A soldier or sailor could be flogged or subjected to other punishment simply on the say-so of a superior officer. In the next chapter, we will see what could result from this state of affairs and how men could be crippled or killed in an alarmingly informal fashion.

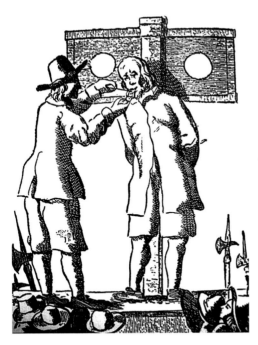

1. The public mutilation and branding with red-hot irons of a blasphemer during the rule of Oliver Cromwell.

2. Libelling the monarch in Elizabethan England could result in having the right hand chopped off.

3. A contemporary drawing of the origin of torture in Britain; a reluctant suspect is handed a red-hot iron bar, which he must carry for nine paces.

4. Calling upon God to decide innocence or guilt; the ordeal by cold water.

5. The subject of 1,000 cartoons.

6. Being married to the Duke of Exeter's daughter; the rack in action in the Tower of London.

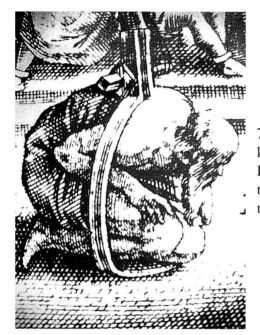

7. Skeffington's Gyves, otherwise known as the Scavenger's Daughter; the opposite procedure to the rack, it squashed, rather than stretched, the victim.

8. Breaking on the wheel was a brutal death. It was occasionally inflicted in Scotland, but never in England.

9. Although never popular in England, thumbscrews were used in Scotland under a variety of names, such pilliwinks.

10. The *peine forte et dure* in action; a torture which was used in Britain well into the eighteenth century on those who refused to enter a plea when brought to trial.

11. Matthew Hopkins, the self-styled 'Witchfinder General'; a man who was ready and willing to use torture in pursuit of the Devil's agents.

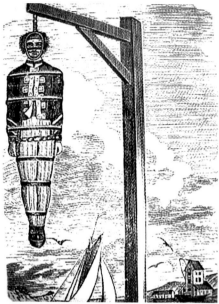

12. Slaves in British colonies were treated like cattle, being branded and whipped at the will of their 'owners'.

13. Gibbetting alive (hanging a man in chains to die of exposure and thirst), was used in both England and the Caribbean.

14. Luisa Calderon was a 15 year-old girl tortured at the orders of the British general, Thomas Picton.

15. Another death by torture; Sir John Oldcastle being roasted over a slow fire. Burning to death could be prolonged in this way for hours.

16. An early example of a man being disembowelled as part of the punishment known as hanging drawing and quartering.

17. The pillory sometimes amounted to being stoned to death; a slow and painful end.

18. An unpleasant and hazardous way of torturing women; deaths were not unknown in the ducking stool.

19. A prisoner after being flogged in the 1860s; this type of torture lingered on in England for another century.

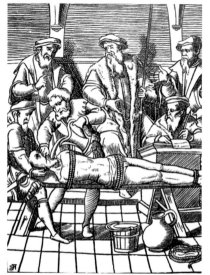

20. Medieval waterboarding. Precisely the same torture was being used by the British Army in Northern Ireland as late as the 1970s.

Chapter 7

Torture in the British Army and Navy

The British Army has a long tradition of using torture to extract information from suspects. This tradition was still going strong well into the twentieth century, as late as the 1970s, in fact. The final chapter of this book will detail the use of torture in Ireland during the insurrection commonly known as 'The Troubles'. On its own men though, torture was used by the army and the Royal Navy, almost exclusively as a means of punishment, rather than during questioning and interrogation.

The history of torture used as punishment in the British Army really only dates from the seventeenth century. Up until that time, there was only one penalty for soldiers who deserted, struck their superiors or looted from the civilian population; they were hanged or shot. This was much the same in ordinary court cases in civilian life, where picking pockets or forging cheques merited the death penalty. We see an example of how indiscipline was dealt with during the medieval period in Shakespeare's *Henry V*, when Bardolph is caught looting after the siege of Harfleur and is summarily executed. This may be a fictional account, but it was true to life.

Of course, executing any soldier who put a foot out of line had the effect of depriving the army of men. It was essentially counter-productive, but with ferocious penalties used against those in ordinary society, it seemed logical to extend the same punishment to those in the armed forces. As civil society changed though, with other punishments besides hanging becoming available, the army too altered its approach. The trend moved away from executions and towards simply inflicting severe pain on recalcitrant men and hoping that this would be sufficient to deter them from misbehaving in the future. This change in attitude towards punishment became formalized after the establishment of a standing army in England during the seventeenth century. In 1689 the Mutiny Act was passed, which set out the use of corporal punishment in the army. For almost 200 years after the passing of this act, British soldiers were liable to be flogged, in some cases to death, for the most trivial offences.

The main method used to punish soldiers as executions became less frequent was flogging. This could, as we shall see, also end in the death of the victim, although this was relatively rare. What flogging did do was to cause the most severe pain imaginable and so it certainly qualifies as torture, at least according to the dictionary definition at which we looked in the introduction to this book.

Before examining in detail how the army and navy used flogging to keep order for the better part of 200 years, we might glance at one or two other ways of torturing men as punishment which were found to be efficacious in the army.

Some highly unusual methods were devised in both the army and navy for inflicting pain on soldiers and sailors who stepped out of line. Some of these tortures are similar to those used elsewhere, but one or two are unique to the armed forces. We shall begin with an unusual means of hurting, and even on occasion killing, offenders. This was known as tying neck and heels.

The practice of tying neck and heels arose separately in Britain and the Indian subcontinent. In nineteenth-century India, a torture called *anundal* was used. This entailed tying up a prisoner into an awkward or painful posture and leaving him to reflect. Often, the feet would be tied together and then a rope passed from the feet and looped around the victim's neck. This would then be pulled very tight and secured. Depending upon the severity of this method, it sometimes resembled the torture of Skeffington's Gyves, at which we looked in Chapter 1. The British Army found this a very useful punishment, because it required no preparation nor did it need anything in the way of special devices.

For tying a man neck and heels, the only equipment necessary was two muskets and a couple of stout straps. The soldier to be punished was compelled to kneel on the ground, with a musket placed beneath his shins. He was then forced to crouch down, with his chest pressed against his thighs. A second musket was placed over the man's neck and then straps were used to pull the two weapons together as tight as could be. The result was that the person was squashed up very tightly, with hardly enough room to breathe. An early-nineteenth-century source describes the effects of this punishment, which was often used informally as a barrack-room discipline: 'In this situation, with his chin between his knees, has many a man been kept until the blood gushed out of his nose, mouth and ears, and ruptures have also been too often the fatal consequences.' It is strange to reflect that 200 years after the use of Skeffington's Gyves was forbidden by the highest court in the land as being inhuman, an informal version such as this, which actually resulted in the death of some victims, was still being used in the British Army.

The ruptures which sometimes resulted from tying a recalcitrant soldier neck and heels could result in death or permanent disability. This was not the only form of torture used by the army which was capable of causing such serious injuries. One method used up until the nineteenth century had originally been used in the torture chambers of the Spanish Inquisition, which accounts for one of the names by which it was known, the Spanish Donkey. In the British Army, it was more commonly known as 'riding the wooden horse' or 'straddling the timber mare'. Writing in the late eighteenth century, Francis Grose gave a detailed account of how this terrible device was constructed and the mode of its use:

Riding the wooden horse was a punishment formerly much in use, in different services. The wooden horse was formed of planks nailed together, so as to form a sharp ridge or angle, about eight or nine feet long. This ridge represented the back of the horse; it was supported by four posts or legs, about six or seven feet long, placed on a stand made moveable by trucks; to complete the resemblance, a head and tail were added.

When a soldier or soldiers were sentenced by a court-martial, or ordered by the commanding officer of the corps, to ride this horse, for both were practised, they were placed on the back with their hands tied behind them, and frequently, to increase the punishment, had muskets tied to their legs, to prevent, as it was jocularly said, their horse from kicking them off; this punishment was chiefly inflicted on the infantry, who were supposed to be unused to ride. At length, riding the wooden horse having been found to injure the men materially, and sometimes to rupture them, it was left off.

The wooden horse gives us another example of how the myth has grown up over the years that torture has never been officially used in Britain. In this case, by changing the terminology a little and adding a ridiculous element, the make-believe head and tail of a horse, we are supposed to see this punishment as a mild and faintly absurd one, the aim being to humiliate, rather than injure a man. The Spanish Inquisition though did not use this same method merely for the purpose of exposing a man to ridicule; they knew that for a man to be positioned in this way of a sharp wooden ridge, with weights attached to his feet is not only excruciatingly painful, but liable also to cause permanent injury to his body. Like tying neck and heels, riding the wooden horse could and did end up with men having either their genitals or internal organs damaged beyond hope of repair.

The history of torture in Britain is littered with examples of this sort: seemingly innocuous punishments which at first sight appear to be designed for little other than mockery, but are able to maim or kill. The ducking stool was one of these, as was hanging a man up by his wrists for hours at a time. Riding the wooden horse fits into this category. At first sight, it amounts to little more than slight discomfort and being exposed to ridicule. In reality, those subjected to it sometimes ended up as cripples, with terrible ruptures which never healed. It is seldom possible to place the human body under severe strain for protracted periods of time without some ill effect.

Apart from ingenious tortures of the kind discussed above, the British Army relied until 1881 upon another way of inflicting severe pain upon a soldier who stepped out of line or challenged the authority of those above him. This was the cat-o'-nine-tails. The 'cat' and the birch were popular instruments for flogging certain classes of criminals in civilian life. In the army though, both could be awarded for the most trifling offences against military law. Throughout British history, whipping has been used as a judicial punishment, using various implements. The two most common instruments though, eventually became the only ones officially sanctioned. These were the birch and the 'cat'. The 'cat' was applied to the bare back of the victim, who was usually tied to a frame. Typically, a drummer or farrier was employed to strike the blows, because these were likely to be men with strong arms! The birch was a bundle of twigs which was lashed to a rod and applied to the bare backside of both men and boys.

The chief difference between the use of flogging in military and civilian life was the severity of the punishment. Although prolonged floggings had been given to those convicted by ordinary courts in the seventeenth and eighteenth centuries, by the time of the Napoleonic Wars, only a few dozen strokes with the cat were likely to be given. How very different was the situation in the army. According to General Sir James Charles Napier, writing in the early nineteenth century, sentences of 2,000 or 3,000 lashes were not uncommon at the end of the eighteenth century. Because it would be impossible to inflict such a flogging on a man without killing him, the punishment was divided into instalments. A doctor was present and he would halt the flogging if and when he felt that the victim's life was in danger. Then the prisoner would be taken back to his cell and his wounds allowed to heal, until he was ready to endure the next 500 or 1,000 strokes with the 'cat'. This process would be repeated, for weeks if necessary, until the full tally had been delivered.

At the beginning of the nineteenth century, the maximum number of blows that could be delivered with the 'cat' in the army was reduced to 1,000. It need hardly be added that 1,000 strokes with the cat-o'-nine-tails could easily prove fatal. Sometimes, something other than the 'cat' was used in the army and in such cases, the victim could be flogged to death with less than 1,000 strokes. An example from the eighteenth century shows the sort of thing which sometimes happened.

In 1779 Captain Joseph Wall was appointed governor of the island of Goree, off the coast of the present-day African nation of Senegal. Wall was a stern disciplinarian and in the three years that he was governor, he got into the habit of acting ferociously and not bothering over-much with formalities such as courts martial. Shortly before he left the island to return to Britain in 1782, Captain Wall was presented with a petition by some of the soldiers under his command. He was due to sail home the next day, but delayed his departure in order to deal with the matter, not to tackle the complaints made, but rather to punish those who had the temerity to raise objections to his way of running affairs. Wall singled out Sergeant Benjamin Armstrong and claimed that the petition amounted to mutiny and that Armstrong was the ringleader. Because he was in a hurry to sail for England, Captain Wall decided that he would not go to all the trouble of a formal court martial, a decision which was to come back to haunt him. Instead, he simply ordered Sergeant Armstrong to be tied a gun carriage and be given 800 strokes on his back. The punishment was carried out not with the standard cat-o'-nine-tails, but with a piece of rope half an inch thick. Black slaves were employed in flogging the unfortunate Armstrong and to ensure that the flogging was a sound one, a new hand was used every twenty-five blows. Captain Wall threatened those performing the punishment that if they did not strike as hard as they were able, then they would be beaten themselves. According to witnesses, he cried, 'Lay on you black beasts or I'll lay it on you. Cut him to the heart. Cut his liver out.' The day after Sergeant Armstrong was so mercilessly beaten, Captain Wall sailed for England. Four days after he left Goree, Armstrong died of the wounds inflicted upon him. When word reached England, Wall was arrested and charged with murder. He managed to flee to France, where he lay low for eighteen years. On his return to England, he was rearrested, tried for murder and then hanged at Newgate.

That soldiers were, on occasion, literally beaten to death during punishments such as that seen above is beyond doubt, but what of the ordinary flogging with a cat-o'-nine-tails? Is it an exaggeration to call this torture? The easiest way of deciding the point is to read an account by somebody who actually underwent the punishment. In 1831, the British Army was being used in this country for riot control and to put down strikes and incipient revolutions by the Chartists and others. One soldier who was being trained in the methods of crowd control was uneasy about what he might be expected to do on the streets of British cities and so he wrote to the newspapers about his thoughts on the matter. As a result, Alexander Somerville, a trooper in the Scots Greys, was charged with writing a seditious letter and court-martialled. Among other things, he had written 'that while the Scots Greys could be relied upon to put down disorderly conduct, they should never be ordered to lift up arms against the liberties of the country and peaceful demonstrations of the people.'

The charge was found to be proved and Somerville was sentenced to receive 150 lashes with the 'cat'. Somerville described afterwards in horrifying detail, just exactly what it felt like to be flogged with the cat-o'-nine-tails.

> The regimental sergeant-major, who stood behind, with a book and pencil to count each lash, and write its number, gave the command, 'Farrier Simpson, you will do your duty.' The manner of doing that duty is to swing the 'cat' twice round the head, give a stroke, draw the tails of the 'cat' through the fingers of the left hand, to rid them of skin, or flesh, or blood; again to swing the instrument twice round the head slowly, and

come on, and so forth. Simpson took the 'cat' as ordered; at least I believe so; I did not see him, but I felt an astounding sensation between the shoulders, under my neck, which went to my toe nails in one direction, my finger nails in another, and stung me to the heart, as if a knife had gone through my body. The sergeant-major called in a loud voice, 'one.' I felt as if it would be kind of Simpson not to strike me on the same place again. He came a second time a few inches lower, and then I thought the former stroke was sweet and agreeable compared with that one. The sergeant-major counted 'two.' The 'cat' was swung twice round the farrier's head again, and he came on somewhere about the right shoulder blade, and the loud voice of the reckoner said 'three.' The shoulder blade was as sensitive as any other part of the body, and when he came again on the left shoulder, and the voice cried 'four,' I felt my flesh quiver in every nerve, from the scalp of my head to my toe nails. The time between each stroke seemed so long as to be agonising, and yet the next came too soon.

This is the effect that just four strokes with the 'cat' had upon a man. Imagining this agony being multiplied by hundreds in the case of a soldier due to receive 1,000 lashes leaves us in no doubt that this was indeed a form of torture.

After the Battle of Waterloo, which marked the end of the Napoleonic Wars, there was increasing disquiet about the routine use of such savage punishments in the armed forces. It would be one thing of the lash were being used only to prevent mutiny and desertion, but this was manifestly not the case. Men were being ferociously tortured for the most trifling of reasons. A riddle of the time sums the case up neatly; 'Why is a soldier like a mouse? Because he lives in terror of the cat.' It was not unknown for 200 strokes to be given for being drunk or even appearing on parade with equipment not properly prepared. And even as the Industrial Revolution gained pace and Britain became the most advanced nation in the world, its soldiers were being literally flogged to death.

A shocking case brought matters to a head in 1846. That year, a 27-year-old soldier called Frederick White had an argument with his sergeant. White, a trooper in the 7th Queen's Own Hussars, was court-martialled and subsequently received 150 strokes of the 'cat'. Two weeks later, the previously healthy young man died at Hounslow barracks. The army surgeons swiftly certified his death as being due to natural causes, but before the funeral could take place, the coroner for Middlesex ordered an inquest and second post-mortem. At the second examination, it was found that White's internal organs were engorged with blood and that it was this injury which had most likely caused his death. On 4 August 1846 the jury brought in their verdict, which was to the effect that Frederick White had died as a direct consequence of the flogging he had received.

The idea of men being beaten to death in this way, unofficial death sentences in fact, did not accord with the spirit of the times. It was one thing when this sort of thing had happened during the eighteenth century, but times had changed since then. Within a few years, the practice of administering the cat-o'-nine-tails in the army had fallen into abeyance and in 1881, it was finally banned.

The situation in the navy was always a little different when it came to torturing men and punishing them in ways which would end in their death. Things happened at sea which might have caused raised eyebrows at home. If a naval vessel returned to Portsmouth with one or two men less than it had set out with, well, that was not a matter of great import. In addition to the liberal use of the 'cat', the navy had one or two special punishments of its own which undeniably constituted torture. Perhaps the most famous of these was keelhauling.

Before going any further, it must be noted that the Royal Navy, unlike some other navies such as that of the Dutch, never adopted keelhauling as a formal punishment, sanctioned judicially. Nevertheless, the procedure was certainly carried out on British ships and some sailors were killed in the process. Keelhauling probably grew from milder forms of discipline, like dunking a man in the sea as scolds were sometimes dipped in village ponds, using special ducking stools. This can be unpleasant and humiliating, but is perhaps not what most people would call 'torture'. A sailor being punished in this way would have a rope looped under his armpits and be lowered into the sea and submerged for a few seconds. At some point, it must have occurred to somebody that the exercise could be more extended and made more gruelling by passing the victim from one side of the ship to the other, by pulling him under the hull or keel of the vessel.

Fully to understand the nature of keelhauling and what it was that made it such a feared ordeal for sailors, it is necessary to know that the hull of a ship below waterline is usually encrusted with barnacles. These are crustaceans which cement hard shells to some fixed object such as a rock. The hard surface of a ship's hull also suits barnacles very well. After a few voyages, the hulls of ships become covered in a layer of barnacles and then have to be scraped clean. If you drag a person over the hull of a barnacle-encrusted ship, then the shells will lacerate the skin in hundreds of places and, in extreme cases, the shock and blood loss alone can cause death. This then was keelhauling, dragging a helpless man under a ship and across a jagged surface.

The method used was typically that the hands and feet would be tied and one long rope secured to the feet and the other the hands. Once this was passed under the ship, it remained only to drop the hapless man into the sea and for the crew to pull on the rope from the opposite side. Sometimes, the victim would drown; more often, he would emerge running with blood and barely able to take breath. A refinement consisted of firing the ship's cannons while he was under water, the booming causing an extra element of terror.

There is no official record of keelhauling on British ships, although accounts of the practice in the seventeenth century certainly exist. Most likely, it was carried out on the whim of a captain, without the formality of a court martial. When a ship of the Royal Navy was thousands of miles from Britain, perhaps sailing across a remote corner of the Pacific Ocean, things might be done which would not be countenanced a few miles from Portsmouth, say. There is little doubt that summary executions did take place at times and there are reliable accounts too of keelhauling being carried out.

Another specifically nautical form of torture was starving a man to death. This was a prescribed punishment for repeated offences of falling asleep on duty. It was essentially a version of gibbeting alive, a practice we saw being used on black slaves in the West Indies. We know that this penalty existed in the British navy, because it is detailed in the *Black Book of the Admiralty*, a collection of the medieval laws relating to crimes at sea. This compilation dates from the fourteenth century and sets out plainly what would befall a sailor who kept falling asleep when he should have been on watch and looking out for any threats to the vessel. Falling asleep on guard duty in this way has always been looked upon as a very serious offence, imperilling as it did not just the individual soldier or sailor himself, but also his comrades in arms. According to the *Black Book*, a first offence of falling asleep on watch would result in a bucket of seawater being poured over the offender's head. For a second offence, the man's arms would be lifted above his head and a bucket of seawater would be poured down each sleeve. So far, these punishments could hardly have been lighter, certainly nothing which would merit the description of 'torture'. In the case of the man caught sleeping a third time, he was tied to the mast with heavy weights secured to his arms. This was uncomfortable, but hardly very painful. It was in the rare event of a man who did not profit from these warnings that the ultimate deterrent came into play.

If any sailor should be found asleep on duty a fourth time, then the punishment was that he should be enclosed in a large basket, along with a loaf of bread, a mug of ale and a sharp knife. The basket was then to be suspended from the bowsprit, so that it was hanging above the sea. An armed sentry was set, to ensure that there could be no possibility of the offender being able to escape and perhaps clamber back on board the ship. From then on, the man in the basket had two choices. He could either eat the bread and drink the ale and then quietly die of hunger and thirst or, if he preferred a quicker death, he could use the knife to cut the basket loose, thus falling into the sea to drown. In effect, this was a death sentence, just another version of being gibbetted alive.

We have seen that instruments of torture were sometimes given female designations; specifically, they were referred to in terms of daughters. The rack was called the 'Duke of Exeter's Daughter' and Skeffington's Gyves were also known as the 'Scavenger's Daughter'. No doubt a psychiatrist would be able to explain this need to connect torture with female nomenclature in this way! We see the same thing in naval punishments which involved a lot of pain. The cat-o'-nine-tails was sometimes known to sailors as the 'Captain's Daughter' and a particularly awful ritual flogging was termed, 'kissing the Gunner's Daughter'.

There was in the eighteenth and nineteenth centuries a tradition of taking youngsters on as sailors. Sometimes, these boys might only be 11 or 12. There was also a category of junior officer known as midshipmen, some of whom could be as young as 13. For these children and teenagers, the discipline could be absolutely ferocious and they were, if they were not careful, likely to find themselves 'kissing the Gunner's daughter'. This meant being tied to a cannon with their trousers down and flogged on their bare bottom with a cat-o'-nine-tails. It might appear to us almost unbelievable, but it was commonly accepted that a teenager could in this way be given dozens of strokes with the 'cat'.

If being flogged with the 'cat' on the back and shoulders was painful, it is difficult to know how it felt to be whipped in this way on the backside. These punishments must have left the victims incapacitated. Some examples will make this clearer. Throughout the nineteenth century, the Admiralty was required to submit annual punishment reports to Parliament. There was, as we have seen, uneasiness about flogging in the army and Parliament wished to know precisely what was happening on this front in the navy, as well as the army. The 1854 report shows every ship of the Royal Navy and how many floggings were carried out on boys and young man. It makes for shocking reading, not so much for the frequency of the whippings, but for their severity. On HMS *Albion*, for instance, there had been just five floggings in 1854, for offences ranging from theft to indecency. The total number of lashes given in those punishments was 204. This means that every one of those boys received an average of over forty lashes with the 'cat' on his bare backside. For a grown man, this would be hideous, but for a boy of 14 or 15, it would be unimaginably awful.

Flogging in the navy was a highly ritualized affair, whether for boys or men. When boys were to be flogged, all the youngsters on board were mustered to witness the punishment. This was thought to have a salutary effect on their future behaviour, the same principle which lay behind the public executions which were a feature of the first half of the nineteenth century in Britain. In theory at least, men were not supposed to be able to watch when a boy was made to 'kiss the Gunner's Daughter', but there are accounts of the older men climbing into the rigging in order to get a good view!

The boy was secured lengthways along the barrel of the cannon, with his backside conveniently positioned so that it was sticking out at the breech. Sometimes, rather than the full-sized cat-o'-nine-tails used for adults, a smaller version of the 'cat' would be wielded, one with only five tails, which was popularly known among the boys by the diminutive 'pussy', to distinguish it from the real 'cat'. A refinement of cruelty is that there was a tradition, not always adhered to, that the boy should be ordered to make the cat-o'-nine-tails which was to be used on him, himself. So before suffering, he would be compelled to sit patiently, twisting ropes and attaching them to the rod.

One feature of the punishment of 'kissing the Gunner's Daughter', was unique and served to distinguish it from adult floggings. Most judicial whippings were undertaken swiftly, with the blows struck as rapidly as the man wielding the 'cat' or birch could manage. Sometimes, in the army, the punishment was made worse by having the lashes struck in time with a drum beat. The drummer would set up a steady rhythm, perhaps striking the drum every two seconds. This meant that the victim would have time to be aware of the pain for a second or two, before having his contemplation interrupted by the next stroke. By all accounts, this had the effect of making a flogging considerably worse, by introducing an element of mental torment, rather akin to the so-called 'Chinese water torture'. As readers perhaps know, the agony in that case was the remorseless dripping of the water on the forehead and having to wait for each drop to fall at regular intervals.

It might have been thought that nothing could have been worse for a teenage boy than to receive dozens of lashes with a cat-o'-nine-tails to his bare bottom, but the process was rendered even more disagreeable, by leaving a space of ten or fifteen seconds between each blow. This meant that delivering forty-eight strokes with the 'cat', the maximum allowed in the mid-nineteenth century, could take twelve minutes. It is hard to imagine carrying out such a protracted and inhuman procedure on a grown man, but these were boys, some as young as 12 or 13.

The severity and duration of 'kissing the Gunner's Daughter' varied greatly, according to what offence was involved and whether the punishment was imposed informally or as a result of a court martial. At one end of the scale, only two or three lashes were given. Writing of his life as a Midshipman in the late eighteenth century, a retired naval officer described the ritual;

> Youth often runs wild and riotous, and requires a tight hand to keep it within bounds. On board the *Mediator*, all these punishments were inflicted at various times; and one morning after breakfast, while at anchor in St John's Road, Antigua, all the midshipmen were sent for into the Captain's cabin, and four of us were tied up one after the other to the breech of one of the guns, and flogged upon our bare bottoms with a cat-o'-nine-tails, by the boatswain of the ship; some received six lashes, some seven, and myself three. No doubt we all deserved it, and were thankful that we were punished in the cabin instead of upon deck, which was not uncommon in other ships of the fleet.

In sharp contrast were two cases of flogging which followed courts martial, one in 1813 and the second in 1822. In the earlier instance, 17-year-old Valentine Woods stabbed one of his shipmates and the court martial ordered that he should receive sixty strokes of the cat-o'-nine-tails on his 'bare posteriors'. This proved to be one of those awful incidents where the punishment had to be delivered in instalments, the victim being unable physically to endure the entire sentence at one go. The Captain's Log of the HMS *Zealous* for 17 July 1813 gives the details;

> at 11.15 Punished Valentine Woods (Boy) with 36 lashes for stabbing John Good, Ships Corporal, being part of his Punishment by sentence of a Court Martial on the 20th day of May 1813

Ten days later, on 27 July, was a second entry relating to the matter;

> At 10, Punished Valentine Woods (Boy) with 24 lashes for stabbing John Good, Ships Corporal, being the remainder part of his Punishment by sentence of a Court Martial held on the 20 May 1813.

That the youth should have had to wait two months between being sentenced by the court martial and actually being flogged, is bad enough. That after receiving thirty-six lashes of the 'cat', he was then obliged to spend ten days recovering from this first flogging sufficiently, so that he could be given another two dozen strokes, is appalling.

The second incident at which we will look was even more serious, because it could have been a capital charge, putting one of the parties to the offence in peril of being hanged. On 11 November 1822, a court martial took place in HMS *Albion,* which was anchored in Portsmouth Harbour. On trial were Private William Osborne, a marine, and 14-year-old William Webber, a crewmember of HMS *Shamrock.* The grown man and teenage boy spent the night together in an otherwise empty cabin and they were discovered the following morning in, 'a very indecent and unclean attitude'. In short, they had been having sex together. A key point of the trial was whether or not there was any evidence of sodomy, because that would have made the matter a capital crime, punishable by a mandatory death sentence. The prosecution at the court martial conceded that there was insufficient evidence to proceed on such a charge. As it was, there was enough to indicate that indecent conduct had taken place. The verdict of the court martial was that:

> the said William Osborne to receive fifty Lashes on his bare back with a Cat O'nine Tails and the said William Webber to receive thirty six Lashes

in the usual Way of punishing boys, on board His Majesty's said Sloop *Shamrock* and both to be mulcted of all wages due and to be dismissed the service.

We have ended by examining one or two cases of boys being flogged in this way with the cat-o'-nine-tails to show once again that even when an action is not actually designated as being torture, it can, by its very nature, be said to amount to it. In the next chapter we shall be looking at how the British spread the idea of torture around the world, until it became an integral part of the most extensive empire the world has ever seen.

Chapter 8

Torture in the British Empire

Torture, other than flogging with the cat-o'-nine-tails or birch, had all but disappeared from Britain by the nineteenth century. Sometimes those being questioned about a crime would be punched or otherwise assaulted but that was the limit of it. But in British possessions overseas, the situation could hardly be more different. From the acquisition of the first colonies in the early seventeenth century until the return of Hong Kong to Chinese sovereignty in 1997, Britain managed its empire effectively by using the time-honoured principle of divide and rule. This was no haphazard and accidental arrangement. Wherever the British occupied some geographical area and absorbed it into their empire, they took steps to ensure that the indigenous inhabitants would spend more time squabbling with each other than they would in uniting against the foreign power which had taken over their homeland. In Palestine, they set Arab against Jew, in Cyprus, Greek against Turk, in India, Muslim against Hindu, in Ireland, Catholic against Protestant and in that part of West Africa that they named Nigeria, the British exacerbated local disputes so that the Yoruba were against the Igbo and the Hausa against them both.

The arrangement of having mutually-hostile groups within one territory meant that often the enforcement of law and, when necessary military subjugation, could be carried out by troops and police who were not actually British themselves. In Cyprus, for instance, Turkish police were recruited who were very keen to crack down hard on Greek nationalists. In Nigeria, Hausa troops could be used to suppress any unrest among the Yoruba. Apart from the obvious advantage of preventing the natives from uniting to drive out the British colonialists, there was another useful aspect of this method of imperial rule. By the beginning of the eighteenth century, it was an established part of the British psyche that torture had no place in their judicial system. The belief that both common law and Magna Carta forbade the use of torture was widespread and this rejection of the practice was a matter of some pride in Britain. It was contrasted in the minds of many British people with the widespread tradition of torture in the rest of Europe. That their nation did not countenance the torture of suspects was seen as an indication of the superiority of the Anglo-Saxon system over that of most of the rest of the world.

As the British Empire became established, it was necessary to provide some justification for the wholesale grabbing of other people's land and the idea took hold that this was in some way a benevolent enterprise, that the British were bringing the benefits of civilization to those who would otherwise live savage and unenlightened lives. Now part of this process of bringing light into the darkness of Asia and Africa consisted of doing away with arbitrary rule and introducing the rule of law, the sort of 'British Values' of which the present government makes so much, in fact. This put colonial administrators in a tricky position, because it is virtually impossible for a foreign invader to maintain order in an undeveloped country without resorting to things such as torture and summary justice. The solution to this conundrum, the need for torture and the desire also to avoid being seen to use it, was a marvellous example of the British genius for compromise; torture would be tolerated, but only if it was carried out by foreigners in the pay of the British! Wherever possible, foreigners should be the ones actually carrying out the abuse of suspects. They could, if anybody enquired, be disowned and even punished for obeying the orders of their British masters and carrying out the torture. Ideally, members of one ethnic group would be encouraged to act against another group, for whom they had some historical animosity. This would make them all the keener to hurt and humiliate their victims. The Mediterranean island of Cyprus during the 1950s, when Britain was fighting one of her last colonial wars against a Greek resistance movement which wished to see Cyprus leave the British Empire, provides us with a perfect example of how this worked.

For centuries, the island of Cyprus was shared between Greek Christians and Turkish Muslims. When the British acquired the territory in 1878, following the end of the Russo-Turkish War, Greeks formed the majority of Cyprus's inhabitants. The last thing that the British wished was for the Turks and Greeks to get along well, because then both groups might come to the conclusion that they could run the country as well or better, without British overlords! In 1955, when some of the Cypriot Greeks began a guerrilla campaign, aimed at forcing Britain to leave Cyprus, the colonial forces on the island felt that they needed to use torture on their prisoners to find out more about the rebellion which they faced. It would hardly have been politic for them to inflict torture themselves. Back home in Britain, ordinary people had been sickened by the excesses of the Third Reich during the Second World War, which had only finished ten years earlier.

The Greek Cypriot guerrilla movement was called EOKA and their aim was simple; to force *Enosis* or union with Greece. This would have transformed Cyprus into no more than a province of Greece. At that time, 20 per cent of those living in Cyprus were Turkish Muslims and they feared, with some justification, that if their country became part of Greece, then they would find themselves reduced to the status of second-class citizens in their own country. There was, as they say today, a lot of 'history' between Greece and Turkey. The prospect for the Turkish Cypriots if their country was absorbed by Greece would not have been brilliant. The British realized this perfectly well and exploited the situation for their own ends.

As we noted above, the British liked to recruit as many of the native population as possible into the police and armed forces of the countries which they occupied. Cyprus was no exception and since the main focus of discontent in the country was among the Greeks, it was only natural they should wish to have a lot of Turks in the police to deal with them. Few of the British administrators had troubled to learn Greek, which meant that they were at a disadvantage when interrogating suspected insurgents. They also, of course, wished to keep their hands clean and not been seen to be mistreating or assaulting their prisoners. This was left to the Turks, who made up the majority of the Special Branch of the police in Cyprus. For the British, it was a perfect arrangement. The Turkish police officers certainly got results and it was the common practice for the British officers to leave prisoners alone with the Turks if they thought that torture was likely to take place.

Adrian Walker, who was an NCO in the Intelligence Corps, wrote years later of the fact that torture by the police had been widespread and common during the EOKA insurgency. He said:

> It would be dishonest of us to gloss over the fact that torture was used extensively in Cyprus to extract information from suspected terrorists or their sympathisers. It was an open secret and very well-known to those of us who served there during the EOKA conflict. Interrogations were often carried out by the Special Branch of the Cyprus police, largely made up from the Turkish community, but with British officers in charge.

Walker tells of the time when the British had had no success in getting a suspect to talk and so decided to hand him over to Turkish members of the Special Branch. After there had been some, 'rough handling', the Greek man was ready to tell the British what they wished to know.

It is impossible now to know the type and degree of the torture to which Greek EOKA members and sympathisers suffered during the guerrilla war in Cyprus, which lasted from 1955 to 1960. Claims and counter-claims were made by all parties in the struggle. What cannot be in any doubt though is that torture *was* used, even if it amounted to no more than what was euphemistically described as 'rough handling', in other words, being beaten up in the cells of a police station. Even the courts at the time, presided over by British colonial judges, began to show unease at the confessions which they were invited to accept as having been freely made.

In May 1957 Sir Paget Bourke, the Cyprus Chief Justice, allowed the appeal of a man called Charalambos Chrisdodoulides, who had been convicted of involvement with EOKA based entirely on a confession which had supposedly been made freely. For Sir Paget Bourke, the fishy part of the business was that the prosecution refused to say who had been interrogating Chrisdodoulides and therefore nobody could swear in court as to what had happened when he was being questioned. Chrisdodoulides said that he had been thoroughly and expertly beaten, until he could stand no more and agreed to sign a statement prepared by the police. This case had already become a scandal in Britain and was raised in Parliament by MP Francis Noel-Baker. On 8 March 1957, he named Sub-Inspector Ismail Hassan, a Turkish police officer, as having been responsible for the ill-treatment of prisoners.

Writing in *Fighting EOKA: The British Counter-Insurgency Campaign on Cyprus, 1955-1959,* David French says that the authorities in Cyprus 'did turn a blind eye to the use of torture in some interrogations', although he suggests that this might not have been as common as EOKA claimed. The insurgency in Cyprus illustrates beautifully the classic tactics of using those of other nationalities to do the 'dirty work'. They could, after all, be disowned if their actions came to light. In this way, the British were able to maintain the illusion that torture was a distasteful, foreign habit that they had been trying to suppress. No better example of how this trick was worked may be found than the Indian subcontinent, which until 1948 included not only India, but also the modern-day countries of Pakistan and Bangladesh.

India was, by the nineteenth century, the most populous of the British colonies. The various principalities and kingdoms which made it up had been able to run their own affairs perfectly well before Britain began to take over. The colonization of India was undertaken by proxy, using a private company which was, nominally at least, operating on behalf of the British government. The East India Company was immensely powerful and rich and had twice as many men under arms as the British Army had at its disposal. It also ran its own navy. Having once gained a foothold in India, its influence expanded rapidly, until it ran much of the country. Now there was in India no tradition of rejecting torture as being unethical. It was in regular use for all sorts of purposes, ranging from the interrogation of prisoners to persuading reluctant businessmen to hand over the taxes which they owed. As British rule became more and more widespread across the subcontinent, it was found to be convenient to leave local customs, such as torturing people to make sure that they settled their tax bills promptly, largely alone. After all, India was a long way from England and as long as nobody back home got to hear of it, there was no reason not to make use of the Indian ways of doing things when it came to law enforcement and financial matters.

Before looking at the most famous case where such practices came to light, let us look at one or two methods of torture which were peculiar to India, although they have their counterparts in English history. One of these was called *anundal*. It needed no equipment more complicated than a length of rope. The head of the person to be tortured by *anundal* might be forced down and tied by a rope to the feet, while the victim was in a squatting position. Readers will remember the old army punishment of being tied neck and heels; this operated on precisely the same principle. It was also similar to Skeffington's Gyves. Alternatively, the arms might be forced high up behind the person's back and secured there for hours with ropes. Another specialized form of torture was known as *kittee*.

Applying pressure to the certain parts of the body has always been known in Europe to be a very effective means of persuading somebody to say what you wish or do as you require. One thinks of the thumbscrews, which were as popular in seventeenth-century Scotland as they were in Nazi Germany. The Indian version was made of wood and astonishingly versatile, not being limited to a specific part of the anatomy as were the thumbscrews. There were two types of *kittee*. One was similar to a lemon-squeezer and consisted of two wooden plates which could be clamped around parts of the body such as the fingers, nose, nipples or external genitals of men. The other type was larger, being two boards which could be fastened around a hand or foot to apply a greater area of pressure and so increased amount of pain.

We mentioned *anundal* earlier and we turn now to an example of its use, one which resulted in the death of a man subjected to it, which came to light during an investigation into torture in the Indian state of Madras in 1855, almost a century after the British presence there had been established. The background to the enquiry into the use of torture is interesting. In 1846, an Englishman called Mr Theobald, who was a barrister in Calcutta, was travelling through Bengal when he was robbed of a bag containing 400 rupees. The thief was soon caught and the local chief of police, an Indian, offered to torture him in front of Mr Theobald. This horrified him so much that he wrote to friends back in England about the affair. The India Reform Society, who opposed the East India Company's monopoly in India, became involved and after many delays, a commission in Madras was set up to investigate how torture was being officially used in India. So keen were people to testify to the commission, that one man walked 1,000 miles to give evidence. The staggering amount of testimony gathered, left little doubt that torture was routinely used by Indian officials acting on behalf of the Englishmen who actually ran the country. Many cases of *anundal* were mentioned, including the following instance.

A man called Vencatachela Rajaulee owed 10 rupees in taxes and the local tax collector was quite determined to make sure that he paid up. Both Rajaulee and his elderly father were seized and tortured. To quote the report prepared after the commission in Madras had completed its work, the two men were;

placed in *anundal,* their legs tied together and their heads tied to their feet in a stooping posture; their hands were tied behind them, and stones placed upon their backs; in which posture they were made to stand from six in the morning until noon. It will hardly be a matter of surprise that the father died the following month.

When the Torture Commission Report was published in 1855, it caused a terrible shock in Britain. Attempts were made to explain away the horrible things documented by blaming the Indians themselves for what had been going on. After noting, correctly, that torture had been in use before the British arrived in India, the report went on to say:

> So deep rooted, however, has the evil been found, and so powerful the force of habit, arising from the unrestrained licence exercised in such acts of cruelty and oppression under the former rulers of this country, that it has not been practicable, notwithstanding the vigorous measures adopted, wholly to eradicate it, from the almost innate propensity of the generality of native officers in power to resort to such practices on the one hand, and the submission of the people on the other; and accordingly the abuse still prevails in the Police Department, although undoubtedly not to the same extent as formerly.

In other words, the British had been trying to put a stop to it, but the Indians themselves were so keen on torturing people that it had so far been impossible to get them to give up the practice!

Before we see why this idea was a pretty feeble one, designed to exculpate the British administration and the men of the East India Company, it might be interesting to look at some of the techniques listed in the report of torture in Madras;

> Twisting rope around the arm to impede circulation; lifting up by the moustache; suspending by the arms tied behind the back; searing with hot irons; placing scratching insects, such as the carpenter beetle, in the navel, scrotum and other sensitive places; dipping in wells and rivers until the party is half-suffocated; beating with sticks; prevention of sleep; nipping the flesh with pincers; putting peppers and chillies in the eyes, or introducing them into the private parts of men and women.

The methods listed above are mostly familiar; some of them had been the stock-in-trade of the Spanish Inquisition for centuries. Suspending a person from the hands, which have been tied behind the back, for instance, was known in the seventeenth century as the *strappado*. Others, like submerging people in water, were popular in Britain, both as a means of testing if a subject was a witch and also as a punishment in itself, known as 'ducking'. The Indians had one or two unusual ways of torturing people though, such as *anundal* and *kittee*, at which we have also looked.

Fully to understand how duplicitous the British were being in this matter, it is necessary now to jump back in time some way from the commission which investigated torture in Madras and see what was happening in the country some sixty years earlier. The reason for proceeding in this way, rather than following a strict, chronological sequence in looking at this subject will soon become apparent.

Anybody reading about the shocking behaviour of the Indian police in Madras in the 1840s and 1850s might be forgiven for thinking that this was some scandal which had been uncovered and that as soon as it had been brought to light, steps would have been taken to curtail the abuses which were revealed. This certainly was how the matter was presented to the British public, and the colonial authorities in India emerged, by and large, as innocent and unwitting parties to cruelty being carried out by the natives without the knowledge or consent of the British.

In 1785, seventy years before the publication of the Madras Torture Commission report, the man who had been appointed the first Governor-General of India returned to Britain. For twelve years Warren Hastings had governed large swathes of India both for the East India Company and also for the British Crown. Two years after his return from India, Hastings was arrested by Parliament's Serjeant-at-Arms and taken to the House of Lords to hear a list of charges made against him, relating to his time as Governor-General of India. He was impeached and ordered to stand trial before Parliament. On 13 February 1788, the trial of Warren Hastings began in Westminster Hall. Although he was being tried by the House of Lords, the members of the Commons were also present to see the start of the proceedings. So much was alleged about the period when Hastings ruled India, that it took Edmund Burke, who was prosecuting, four days just to read out all the charges!

Hastings stood accused of many different things, ranging from arbitrary executions to enriching himself personally through corrupt activity. One of the things of which he was suspected was countenancing, and even encouraging, torture, particularly by tax collectors. This accusation tied in neatly with the idea that Hastings was a grasping and rapacious man, eager to enrich himself by any means.

A good deal of what Edmund Burke alleged is not germane to the subject of this book, dealing as it did with political matters and the supposed material gain which Warren Hastings made from his position as Governor. However, torture was also suggested to have been undertaken on behalf of Hastings, principally by tax collectors and Parliament was told in great detail what was done to those who would not pay up promptly:

> Those who could not raise the money, were most cruelly tortured: cords were drawn tight round their fingers, till the flesh of the four on each hand was actually incorporated, and became one solid mass: the fingers were then separated again by wedges of iron and wood driven in between them. Others were tied two and two by the feet, and thrown across a wooden bar, upon which they hung, with their feet uppermost; they were then beat on the soles of the feet, till their toe-nails dropped off. They were afterwards beat about the head till the blood gushed out at the mouth, nose and ears; they were also flogged upon the naked body with bamboo canes, and prickly bushes, and, above all, with some poisonous weeds, which were of a most caustic nature, and burnt at every touch. The cruelty of the monster who had ordered all this, had contrived how to tear the mind as well as the body; he frequently had a father and son tied naked to one another by the feet and arms, and then flogged till the skin was torn from the flesh; and he had the devilish satisfaction to know that every blow must hurt; for if one escaped the son, his sensibility was wounded by the knowledge he had that the blow had fallen upon his father : the same torture was felt by the father, when he knew that every blow that missed him had fallen upon his son.
>
> The treatment of the females could not be described: dragged forth from the inmost recesses of their houses, which the religion of the country had made so many sanctuaries, they were exposed naked to public view; the virgins were carried to the Court of Justice, where they might naturally have looked for protection, but now they looked for it in vain; for in the face of the Ministers of Justice, in the face of the spectators, in the face of the sun, those tender and modest virgins were brutally violated. The only difference between their treatment and that of their mothers was, that the former were dishonoured in the face of day, the latter in the gloomy recesses of their dungeons. Other females had the nipples of their breasts put in a cleft bamboo, and torn off. What modesty in all nations most carefully conceals, this monster revealed to view, and consumed by slow fires; nay, some of the monstrous tools of this monster Devi Sing had, horrid to tell, carried their un-natural brutality so far as to drink in the source of generation and life.

There was much more in the same vein and so detailed and similar were the accounts, that it was hardly possible to imagine that it had all been invented.

Another popular torture was also described; one which was well known in Asia, the *falaka*. It is a curious fact that the *falaka*, which consisted of beating men on the souls of their feet with canes, never really caught on in Europe. It is an exquisitely painful experience and if carried out carefully and in moderation, leaves no marks upon the body. It is the perfect method of torture for those who wish later to deny that anything has been done. According to Edmund Burke though, the *falaka*, as practised when Warren Hastings was Governor, was not carried in moderation; far from it. In his speech, he said that those collecting taxes seized the men who claimed to be unable to pay and 'Threw them with their heads downwards over a bar, beat them on the soles of the feet with rattans, until the nails fell from the toes'.

So eloquent and persuasive was Edmund Burke's opening speech that even Hastings himself was hypnotized by it, writing later that, 'for the first half hour, I looked up to the orator in a reverie of wonder, and during that time I felt myself the most culpable man on earth'. Public opinion was at first strongly against the former governor. It was not at all uncommon for officials in remote parts of the British empire to enrich themselves and behave as though they were dictators in their own little kingdoms.

The problem was that the trial dragged on and on, for months and then years. At first, the public were excited to hear all the gory details of what Warren Hastings had supposedly been up to, but as the years passed, there were more interesting news items and far more pressing concerns, the French Revolution, for instance. By the time that the verdict was finally ready to be delivered in April 1795, a third of the lords who were present when the indictment was read had died. After having heard from various officials in India, the House of Lords voted to acquit Hastings of all charges. Far from having profited by his tenure as Governor-General, Warren Hastings was a ruined man, having been obliged to spend every penny he possessed defending himself against the charges. When the trial eventually ground to a halt, he was £70,000 in debt, an astoundingly large sum of money at that time.

It is this which makes the investigation into the use of torture in India in the 1850s so grotesque. However much Warren Hastings did or did not know about the business, there was, in 1795, never any dispute about the fact that the tax collectors and police in British-ruled parts of India were using torture to extract both revenue and confessions. This was reported in the British newspapers and became the theme of general remark. To pretend as the authorities did in 1855, sixty years after the trial of Warren Hastings, that they were astonished to learn that the use of torture was widespread among the police and tax collectors in India simply beggars belief! The only way that the situation could possibly have continued for those decades was if the use of torture was at least tolerated and very likely actively encouraged, by the British rulers of the country.

We move forward another fifty years and see what was happening in India by that time, well over a century since the revelations of torture in that country were the talk of London. In 1908 a woman living in the Punjab region of India poisoned her husband, was arrested, tried and sentenced to death. Gulab Bano, the woman concerned, appealed successfully against her conviction on the grounds that she only confessed to the crime because she had been subjected to the most horrifying torture. A doctor who examined her confirmed that what she alleged had almost certainly happened. Gulub Bano claimed that after her arrest, she had been hung upside down in the police station and a baton smeared with chillies pushed with great force into her anus. We recall what the Madras commission on torture had said in 1855, on the matter of, 'putting peppers and chillies in the eyes, or introducing them into the private parts of men and women'! It seemed that over half a century later, the very same methods were still being used.

Let us fast-forward another forty years until we reach the years that India and Pakistan were granted independence. Activists who had been opposing British rule were circulating accounts, right up until the British withdrew from the country, of 'the application of chilli powder to the genitals of men and women, and anal penetration with a variety of instruments'. It seems that those same methods of torture mentioned from 1795 onwards were still going strong after the end of the Second World War!

When he entered the White House in 2009, one of President Obama's first acts was supposedly to order the removal of a bust of Winston Churchill from the Oval Office. There has been much debate about this, but at the time many people took it to be symbolic of Barack Obama's detestation of the British Empire and all it stood for. There may well have been something in this idea. After all, Obama's own grandfather had been tortured by the British during what was sometimes known as the 'Mau Mau Uprising' in Kenya, during the 1950s. According to his widow, Hussein Onyango Obama had had pins forced under his fingernails and his testicles crushed between two metal rods while he was being interrogated. Two men who were being questioned at the same time had been castrated.

Obviously, during a guerrilla campaign of the sort which took place in Kenya, claims of atrocities are routinely made by both sides and it can sometimes be difficult to untangle falsehood from truth. In the case of the insurgency in Kenya though, there cannot be the least possible doubt that torture was regularly practised against the indigenous inhabitants by British forces, particularly against members of the Kikuyu tribe. We know this, because only a few years ago, the British government was forced to accept responsibility for what had been done in Kenya and to offer an unconditional apology for the whole business.

A minute before midday on 6 June 2013, Foreign Secretary William Hague rose in the House of Commons to make a truly astonishing admission. In a carefully drafted statement, he said;

> The British Government recognise that Kenyans were subject to torture and other forms of ill treatment at the hands of the colonial administration. The British Government sincerely regret that these abuses took place and that they marred Kenya's progress towards independence. Torture and ill treatment are abhorrent violations of human dignity, which we unreservedly condemn.

William Hague was not apologising for something which had taken place in the British Empire centuries before, the slave trade perhaps, or the abuse of natives during the 1857 Indian Mutiny. He was in fact talking about events which happened well within living memory and the speech he made in Parliament was made in part to announce that the British Government had made a settlement with the survivors of the massacres and torture which had been such a feature of colonial Africa as late as the 1950s.

Before we look at the background to the terrible story of what was done in Kenya, perhaps it would be instructive to look at the stories of one or two of the victims. There can be no possible doubt about what was done to these people, it was openly admitted to the House of Commons. Take Paulo Nzili. In 1957, he was arrested and taken to one of the concentration camps which the British had set up to hold those whom they suspected of joining the resistance movement which was then struggling to free Kenya from British colonial rule. He was not a cooperative prisoner and so it was thought that an example should be made of him, to show others what happened to the men who did not play by the rules of the British, who were at that time running the country.

In some ways, Paulo Nzili was lucky. Capital punishment, as well as torture, were being freely used by the British and men were being publicly hanged for crimes as trivial as consorting with men known to oppose British rule. As it was, he was taken out in front of the other prisoners in the camp where he was being held and then stripped naked. In his own words:

> Kwatanehi was told to pin me to the ground. He was a very strong man. He pulled my right arm violently from behind me, through my legs which caused me to somersault over onto my back. They tied both of my legs with chains and Kwatanehi pinned down both of my hands. Luvai then approached me with a large pair of pliers which were more than a foot long and castrated me.

The sheer horror of this account makes any comment superfluous. Nor was it just men who were tortured.

Jane Muthoni Mara was 15 in the mid-1950s, when she was accused of helping the insurgents by supplying them with food. This is how she describes what happened during her interrogation by British soldiers:

> Suddenly there were four guards hovering around me. I was then pinned down to the floor by one man who held my shoulders. Two other men held each arm and one man prised open and held my thighs apart. Edward was sitting on a chair directly in front of my spread legs and was pressing on my bare feet with his spiky army boots.
>
> I was screaming and resisting and trying to wriggle and free myself from the men who were holding me down. Suddenly Edward produced a glass soda bottle. Waikanja told him to push the bottle into my vagina, which he did. I felt excruciating pain and then realized that the glass bottle contained very hot water. I was in so much pain and I could not stop crying and screaming. I felt completely and utterly violated by this sexual torture, but I continued to insist that I had not taken an oath. This lasted for about 30 minutes and was very painful. When I was in the tent, I saw this being done to the other three women.

It is torture of this kind that the Foreign Secretary admitted had been inflicted upon men and women whose only crime was to want to run their own country.

Fully to understand why the British felt obliged to carry out massacres and torture men and women in these disgusting ways, it will be necessary to look a little at the background of Kenya and see what the British were doing in the country in the first place. The Highlands of Kenya, known in colonial times as the 'White Highlands', have very rich soil and a temperate climate which makes it an ideal place for growing coffee. When the British were moving into East Africa, it was hardly surprising that such an ideal location for agriculture should have been seized for the benefit of the Europeans who were taking over the continent. Those living there as independent farmers were either driven out of the area or transformed in wage-slaves, working for the white plantation owners.

As in the other parts of the world that they conquered and occupied, the British relied in Kenya, which was at first known as the East African Protectorate and later the Kenya Crown Colony, upon the time-honoured trick of divide and rule. The main tribe living in the Highlands area, which the British settlers coveted, was the Kikuyu. To subjugate them, the colonists called upon the Masai, who regarded the Kikuyu as their historic enemies and were only too glad to be given the opportunity to torture or massacre them. In this way, the possible threat of unified opposition to the British was neutralized and diverted instead into tribal warfare.

After the end of the Second World War, it seemed to many people living in the British colonies that things must surely change. In Kenya, the Kikuyu began to demand the return of the prosperous 'White Highlands' and, in the long term, independence for their country. None of this endeared them to the British settlers and when in 1952 a guerrilla campaign against the occupying forces was launched, a state of emergency was declared throughout the whole of Kenya. The organization leading the struggle against the British was called the Kenya Land and Freedom Army or KLFA for short. The British though had another name for the insurgents; they called them the Mau Mau. Nobody really knows where the name 'Mau Mau' came from. It was suggested that it might be an anagram of, 'Uma, Uma!', which Kikuyuy boys used to shout at each other during play and meant simply, 'Get out get out!' By this etymology, it might have been a rallying cry aimed at the white settlers who had taken the Kikuyu land.

The most notable feature of the Kenyan Emergency was the sheer savagery displayed by both sides in the struggle. It is perfectly true that the Kikuyu guerrillas indulged in some exceedingly unsavoury practices and that they were responsible for a number of terrible murders, but it is equally true that the British forces were guilty of many atrocities during the campaign to subdue the unrest. We will look at some of the cold-blooded massacres carried out by both sides and the steps which the British took to supress the uprising, but first we must examine the casualty figures and ask just what sort of threat was really posed by the ill-equipped fighters of the Kenya Land and Freedom Army.

A total of 12,893 black Africans died during the Kenyan insurgency, which lasted from 1952 to 1960. During that same period, just 12 white soldiers were killed. True, a few European settlers died as well, 95 of them, but the fact remains that 130 times as many Africans were killed during the 'Mau Mau' campaign as white people. The reasons for this huge disparity was very simple. While the African guerrilla were for the most part armed with machetes and knives, the British were using sophisticated weaponry which included machines guns, mortars and artillery. Even the RAF were part of the effort to crush resistance to colonial rule. Between 18 November 1953 and 28 July 1955 Lincoln bombers of the RAF dropped a total of 50,000 tons of bombs in Kenya.

The subject of this book is of course the use of judicial torture in Britain and its empire and so the wider aspects of the war fought to maintain the British grip on East Africa lies beyond its scope. It has been necessary though to give a brief outline of the position, to place the use of torture in context. One of the things to bear in mind is a point which has already been emphasised: that wherever they colonized, the British had a habit of setting one section of the native population against the other, to ensure that there was no unified uprising against white rule. The Masai were used against the Kikuyu as part of this strategy, but the Kikuyu were also divided against themselves. Some joined the KLFA, while others were recruited by the British into a home guard, which worked alongside the British Army. Those who joined this home guard were seen by some as traitors to their own people and the militants of the KLFA killed many of the home guard and also murdered their families. An incident at the settlement of Lari shows how this sort of conflict could result in the systematic use, by British forces, of torture against civilians.

On the night of 25 March 1953, soon after the start of the so-called 'Mau Mau Uprising', militants from the KLFA attacked a village which was known to be loyal to the British and many of whose men had joined the home guard organised by the British. Over seventy people, a lot of them women and children, were butchered and their homes burned. There was a good deal of mutilation and some of the victims were burned alive. When retaliation came, it was swift, sure and every bit as barbaric as the original massacre. Some supporters of the KLFA, about 150, were murdered and others were taken to police stations, where they were tortured by the British police and their Kikuyu assistants. Some of the worst torture was used on women suspected of helping the KLFA in their attack on Lari. A number of the women were forced to have sex with police dogs, while others had bottles forced into their vaginas, sometimes containing hot water.

It was in the concentration camps set up by the British that some of the worst excesses were committed. These camps were established in remote areas and access was denied to outsiders. The International Committee of the Red Cross, for instance, made repeated requests to the British authorities to be allowed to visit the camps and report on conditions there, but for two years, they were forbidden to enter any of the camps. When, in February 1957, the Red Cross finally reached the camps, they found that illness and malnutrition was rife.

The camps which the British set up to hold those suspected of membership of the KLFA were unbelievably squalid and brutal. Well over 50,000 Africans were detained in these places during the insurgency. They reproduced many of the worst features of notorious German concentration camps such as Belsen and Dachau. It was little wonder that nobody wanted the Red Cross investigating these places. Sanitation was all but non-existent, galvanized steel buckets being the only provision for the bodily needs of those in the crowded camps. In September 1954 one camp, Manyani, had 16,000 prisoners; the conditions, with no access to sanitation and no running water, can only be imagined. The buckets which were used for bodily functions were left standing near the containers of fresh water and it will surprise nobody to learn that a natural consequence was an epidemic of typhoid. There were 1,151 cases at the camp in three months.

Pulmonary tuberculosis was another disease which was common in the Kenyan concentration camps. Prisoners fell victim to this because many were already suffering from deficiency diseases such as scurvy and kwashiorkor. Their resistance to other illnesses was greatly reduced in consequence. Their health was so poor because they were provided with an inadequate diet. In short, the conditions in the camps run by the British in Kenya were very similar to those in the German concentration camps of the 1930s and 1940s, a fact that the British were anxious should not come to light. Fortunately for them, Africa was not Europe and what might have caused outrage in Germany and Poland hardly raised an eyebrow when it took place in a remote part of east Africa.

Much of the torture carried out in Kenya was of an impromptu nature and took place in police stations, soon after a suspect had been captured. This is terrible enough, of course. Men were castrated, women violated, ears sliced off, lit cigarettes pushed into ears and a host of other things done which might encourage people to reveal what the authorities wished to know. That this kind of torture was taking place was known even in the higher echelons of colonial power. It was part of the established armoury of repression at which the British were so adept. Then there was the use of torture in the concentration camps, pain used to persuade people to toe the line and renounce their allegiance to the KLFA. This could be even more brutal than the tricks that the police and army got up to when interrogating newly captured prisoners.

Just as in the camps of Soviet Russia and Nazi Germany, discipline was harsh and unremitting in the British camps in Kenya. Public hangings of those thought to be remaining loyal to the insurgents were not uncommon and the aim of the whole system was to break individuals down and make them conform to the government's ideas of what was an acceptable way to think and live. That the savage treatment in the camps was known at the very highest levels can be seen when we look at the sort of things which the attorney general of the British administration in Kenya was writing to the governor at the time that the torture and ill-treatment in the camps was reaching a crescendo. In 1957 Eric Griffith-Jones, the attorney general, wrote to Governor Evelyn Baring. He explained that it was important that those administering the violence should remain, 'collected, balanced and dispassionate' about what they were doing. On a practical level, he wanted to make sure that beatings were, as a rule, restricted to the upper body, but that it was important that 'vulnerable parts of the body should not be struck, particularly the spleen, liver or kidneys'. The attorney general went on to remind the governor that if they were to sin, then 'we should sin quietly'.

It was perhaps inevitable that when even the top legal authority in the country was happy for torture to be used against detainees that conditions in the camps would not improve and that the brutality would grow steadily worse. After all, if even the governor and attorney general knew what they were up to and approved of it, why should they stop beating and torturing the prisoners? Inevitably, the day came when matters went too far, even for this secluded corner of British imperialism.

Griffith-Jones' remarks about the correct way to torture prisoners were made to the governor in June 1957. Eighteen months later, there was trouble in the Hola camp, where prisoners were refusing to work. One way of wearing down the obstinacy and resistance of the men detained in Hola had been to force them to engage in exhausting, physical labour. They were expected to spend their days digging an irrigation channel with pickaxes and spades. There was passive resistance to this forced labour though and an increasing number of prisoners were simply refusing to pick up their tools and march to work. There was no violence, no shouting or rioting: the men just stood still when the order was given and would not go off with the others to work. By February 1959, this disobedience was spreading. The Senior Superintendent of Prisons in Nairobi visited Hola and advised the camp commandant on how to handle the passive resistance which was now getting out of hand. He left written orders for the response to such disobedience, which stated that the order to pick up tools and march to work should be given and that: 'It is assumed that the party would obey this order, but if they refused, they would be manhandled to the site of the work and forced to carry out the task.' Anybody reading these instructions would probably assume that they had *carte blanche* to do as they pleased to the recalcitrant prisoners and so it proved when the time arrived to put this plan into action.

On 3 March 1959, the prisoners at Hola camp were assembled and ordered to pick up their spades and other tools and march to the irrigation canal which was being dug about a mile from the camp. Some obeyed the instruction, many didn't. When the order was repeated, eighty-eight men simply sat down on the ground and refused to move. Whereupon the Commandant gave orders to the guards, who fell upon the prisoners and began swinging pick-axe handles and spades at them. By the time that they had finished, eleven prisoners had been killed and many others seriously injured, some with broken limbs which would never set properly, meaning that they were crippled for life.

Even in such camps, which were known for the routine torture and even murder of prisoners, this was a little much. Various stories were concocted to explain the deaths. A white man who arrived on the scene later that day and enquired about the pile of corpses was told that the men had been overcome with the heat and begun fighting each other, which had caused all the bruises and broken limbs. Then they had fainted and in an effort to revive them, water had been thrown over their faces, which had unfortunately caused them to drown! Even in a country famous for turning the proverbial blind eye to the death of black people, this was a little thin. Still working with the idea of water, a more plausible explanation for the deaths of eleven men was devised. In this version, the men had been poisoned by drinking contaminated water. It was hinted that their own poor standards of hygiene were to blame.

The massacre at Hola was a step to far and word leaked out about it, eventually reaching newspapers in England, following which, questions were asked in Parliament. It would seem hardly possible that the story could get any worse and yet on 4 June 1959, Sir Barnett Stross, MP for Stoke-on-Trent, rose in the House of Commons and asked the Secretary of State for the Colonies;

> How many of the men who died following the use of physical violence in the Hola camp were suffering from scurvy: and to what extent this deficiency disease contributed to their death.

After some obfuscation from the relevant department, the answer which was given made it clear that all the dead men had been suffering from scurvy.

The Conservative administration of Harold Macmillan still hoped desperately that the torture and murder of men thousands of miles away in Africa might somehow be forgotten about, if only MPs would stop asking awkward questions. Fortunately, there were men of principle in Parliament who had no intention of allowing the matter to be brushed under the carpet. One Member of Parliament in particular had no intention at all of allowing such a disgraceful episode to be airbrushed from history.

On 27 July 1959, the member for Wolverhampton delivered what was widely regarded as a masterpiece of Parliamentary rhetoric. There could be no ignoring this speech in the Commons by a rising star of the Conservative Party, a man who had been Junior Housing Minister in 1955 and then, two years later, Financial Secretary to the Treasury. He said:

> We cannot say 'We will have African standards in Africa, Asian standards in Asia and perhaps British standards here at home.' We have not that choice to make. We must be consistent with ourselves everywhere. All government, all influence of man on man, rests on opinion. What we can do in Africa, where we can still govern and where we no longer govern, depends upon the opinion which is entertained of the way in which this country acts and the way in which Englishmen act. We cannot, we dare not, in Africa of all places, fall below our own highest standards in the acceptance of responsibility.

This remarkable piece of oratory, which forced the government to act, was delivered by none other than Enoch Powell, a man whose name was later to become a byword for racial prejudice and intolerance!

After Powell's speech in the Commons, action was finally taken, however inadequate. Two senior officials in Kenya were compelled to retire early, although they did not lose their pensions. It is only in recent years that the full horror of what was done in Kenya during the 1950s has come to light. The treatment of the men and women of the Kikuyu represented the nadir of British administration of her empire, matching any of the awful things done in the eighteenth and nineteenth century.

In this chapter we have looked at the use of torture and murder in three British possessions overseas, one in Europe, one in Asia and the other Africa. It would be possible to examine any number of other territories, from the port of Aden to the island of Zanzibar, but a similar pattern would have emerged, that is to say the regular and systematic use of torture as a tool of government. It was, together with the old principle of divide and rule, an integral and indispensable part of the way of maintaining the largest empire the world has ever seen.

One final point about torture in the British Empire needs to be made. We have seen the Roman dictum of *divide et impera* put into practice, as a way of preventing conquered and occupied nations from uniting against colonial rule. One aspect of this strategy has a direct bearing upon the way in which torture was used in the British colonies and that is that the British themselves were, by and large, able to keep their hands clean. More than that, they managed to make the people whose lands they had seized appear to be cruel savages, in need of the civilizing, British influence! This was no mean feat. The torture of Kikuyu insurgents and the massacre at the concentration camp at Hola in Kenya, were both were carried out not by white people, but by black Africans acting under their instructions.

It was always important for the British that they appeared to be spreading the 'British Values' of the rule of law, democracy and individual liberty around the world; otherwise, what justification might they have for their empire? For this reason, the duty of torturing suspects was generally passed onto the natives. In Cyprus, the Turks were allocated the job, in India, the police and tax gatherers were Indians and in Africa too, it was the indigenous inhabitants who ended up with the task of killing and inflicting brutality.

Our exploration of this topic has now led us to the modern age, the twentieth and twenty-first centuries. In the next two chapters, we will look at the use of pain both as a punishment and also as an aid to interrogation in Britain, culminating in the series of events which led to the United Kingdom being denounced at the European Court of Human Rights as a sponsor of state-sanctioned torture in the questioning of terrorist suspects.

Chapter 9

The Twentieth Century

We are so accustomed today, not only in this country but also in most of the developed world, to the idea that deliberately inflicting pain on another person is utterly wrong and abhorrent, that it is easy to forget that torture was still going strong in Britain for the greater part of the twentieth century and that our modern sensitivity on the matter is a very recent development. Torture, in the sense of the authorized use of severe pain, was in use both as a method of punishment and to obtain information and confessions until well into the 1980s. Indeed, any soldier, police officer or judge from Britain in the mid-twentieth century would feel that he could not do his job properly unless it was accepted that pain had a useful part to play in the investigation of crime and its deterrence. A single statistic might make this clearer. In 1917 alone, 6,135 youths were flogged in England and Wales by order of the courts, chiefly with the birch. More than fifteen young men a day were being sentenced to be flogged and both the 'cat' and birch were being freely imposed by magistrates and judges.

Before looking in detail at the use of whipping as a deterrent in Britain during the last century, let us look at how physical force and the judicious infliction of pain was an integral feature of criminal investigation. The situation today is very plain. If any threat of violence is offered to a prisoner being questioned, then that alone is sufficient to contaminate the case and virtually ensure an acquittal. It is quite enough that the person being questioned has been put in fear of physical assault for any statements made under such duress to be rendered void. The most scrupulous care is taken to ensure that not only is no prisoner struck, but that nobody in custody might be put in a position where they have the least uneasiness about such a thing happening. But it was not always so! We have seen that the interrogation of suspects in foreign countries was frequently accompanied by brutal treatment of a kind which would have raised eyebrows had it been undertaken closer to home. Even so, torture *was* in use in the British Isles, although it was seldom called by its correct name.

Until the 1970s, there was an unspoken assumption by both the police and career criminals that there was likely to be a certain amount of violence by the police in the course of their investigations. Suspects would be knocked around, struck on parts of the body where bruises would not be noticeable, have their arms or ears twisted painfully and generally mistreated until they gave a statement which was acceptable to the police. Generally, but not invariably, the assaults were limited to fists and feet. In some police forces though, pressure to obtain convictions was exerted from above and detectives assured that whatever methods were used, their superiors would protect them. This use of what the Americans call the 'third degree' was less common than simple 'roughing up', but still took place regularly, well into the so-called 'Swinging Sixties'. Sometimes, this sort of thing got out of hand and became torture in all but name.

On 14 March 1963, the police in the Yorkshire city of Sheffield arrested three men for burglary. There was no evidence to connect any of the three men with any crime, nor were they willing to make statements admitting any wrongdoing. At this point, Kenneth Hartley, Albert Hartley and Clifford Bowman might reasonably have expected to receive a few cuffs around the head and maybe a little verbal abuse – such things would have been within the unwritten rules which governed the relations between police officers and professional criminals at that time. In fact, the police in Sheffield had been given explicit instructions that when it came to extracting confessions and getting convictions, no holds were barred. A meeting was held among CID officers, while the three men were in the cells of the police station, and the decision taken to beat a confession out of them and to back up any statement obtained by planting evidence on them as well. Two detectives called Derek Millicheap and Derek Streets were allotted the task of ensuring that the three suspects ended up in court, after admitting that they had been engaged in criminal activity. In fairness to the police officers, they believed that they had been ordered to use violence to obtain confessions.

After planting a screwdriver and a pair of gloves in a van owned by one of the suspects, to suggest that they had been going equipped to steal, Millicheap and Streets began beating the three supposed burglars methodically, applying not only their fists, but also truncheons and a whip made of a rhinoceros tail. Had they not used the truncheons and rhino whip, it is altogether possible that the victims of this sustained assault might have written it off as an occupational hazard, the sort of thing which happened if you fell foul of the police. In the event, they felt so aggrieved that they went to the local newspaper. As a consequence of this, Millicheap and Streets were thrown out of the force. It was at this point that things went seriously wrong for the CID in Sheffield, for the two men appealed against their dismissal, on the grounds that they had only been following orders and it was therefore unjust for them to lose their jobs.

The defence of 'only obeying orders' was of course employed by Nazi war criminals at the Nuremburg trials which were held after the end of the Second World War. It cut no ice then and nor did it when the two disgraced detectives tried it in Sheffield in 1963. It had the effect, though, of bringing to light a culture among the CID of that city which advocated the wholesale torture of suspected criminals as a matter of official policy. This was no case of one or two mavericks, bad apples who had to be rooted out. Despite the efforts of the Chief Constable, Eric Staines, to hush things up, Home Secretary Henry Brooke set up a public enquiry to look into what had been going on. Over the course of twelve days in September 1963, this met at Sheffield Town Hall and some of what came to light seemed almost unbelievable to the average citizen.

Millicheap and Streets told the enquiry that beatings were regularly ordered and that CID officers met in a local pub to plan this sort of systematic violence. Once suspects were under arrest and in the hands of the CID, they were in for a very rough time. Detectives would strip to the waist, so as not to get splashes of blood on their clothing, and then beat those they suspected of crimes mercilessly, until they agreed to sign confessions. A senior detective, Chief Inspector Frederick Rowley, was very candid about the practice. He said, while giving evidence, 'These things go off fairly frequently. You can't have kid gloves on when detecting crime.' The Chief Constable denied knowing anything about it, but Commander Willis, chair of the enquiry, dismissed him as being 'an unconvincing witness'. Both the Chief Constable and the head of the CID in Sheffield were subsequently suspended. Both resigned a few weeks later.

Disturbing though the events in Sheffield were, they had their counterpart in many other parts of Britain at that time. Had the detectives concerned limited themselves to the traditional slapping and twisting of arms, then in all probability nobody would have been any the wiser. Chief Inspector Rowley's remark about not being able to have kid gloves on when detecting crime would have struck a chord with most police officers fifty or sixty years ago. After all, what do you do with somebody you know to be guilty, if he refuses to cooperate?

After what became known as the 'Sheffield Affair', police officers minded to use truncheons or whips to obtain confessions tended, on the whole, to think again. Punching, grabbing, threatening and shaking were still part of the arsenal to harry arrested men into signing incriminating statements, but by and large the violence was more muted and blood was seldom shed. There were of course exceptions, particularly in cases involving terrorists, child molesters or other unpopular types of suspects. Eleven years after the events in Sheffield, Britain was in the middle of a ferocious terrorist campaign of bombings and shootings in English cities, including London and Birmingham.

On 21 November 1974, two bombs exploded in Birmingham. They killed twenty-one people and injured many more. When six Irishmen were picked up, a matter of hours later, the West Midlands police were sure that they had caught the IRA terrorists responsible for the explosions. Because they were confident that they had the right men, the police officers questioning them became so enthusiastic about their task that when the men appeared in court later, they were covered in cuts and bruises. It was alleged that mock executions had been staged and the suspects beaten and burned with cigarettes.

Because of the mood of the times, nobody was unduly worried about the idea of a bunch of bombers being knocked about. After leaving police custody, they were remanded to Winson Green Prison. While there, they received various new injuries. That ordinary people were quite tolerant of violent criminals being mistreated in prisons or police stations may be seen by what happened when fourteen prison officers were later tried for no fewer than ninety separate charges of assault on the suspects. Despite the most damning evidence and a summing-up by the judge which indicated strongly that he himself had no doubt about the treatment meted out to the victims, the jury unanimously acquitted all the prison officers of every charge. Public opinion was, in this case at least, firmly against the victims of cruelty and mistreatment.

After the beating of the Birmingham bombers had passed without anybody being called to account, it must have seemed to the police in that part of the country that they had *carte blanche* to conduct their investigations in any way that they saw fit. It was perhaps this which led detectives in the West Midlands to believe that they could try similar tactics on ordinary criminals. A systematic approach to questioning developed in the heart of England which led to torture being used when professional criminals protested their innocence. Those conducting the torture were members of the West Midlands Serious Crime Squad, which was later disbanded following a serious of horrifying revelations, chief among which was that during questioning, officers were using the sort of techniques more commonly heard of in Third World dictatorships.

In 1980, a career criminal called Keith Twitchell was arrested by the West Midlands Serious Crime Squad and taken to a police station. He was questioned about a robbery in which somebody had died. A Securicor van had been ambushed and one of the guards shot dead. The police invited Twitchell to confess to both the robbery and shooting, which he declined to do. He was in a very vulnerable position. His clothes having been sent for forensic examination, he was naked. When Keith Twitchell persisted in denying any connection with the robbery and shooting, he was seized by eight detectives and forced into a chair, to which he was then handcuffed. After he was secured there, naked, a plastic bag was put over his head and held in place until he began to suffocate. This process was repeated until he passed out. After this, he signed a statement and was only then allowed access to a solicitor. Twitchell heard the detectives who tortured him in this way refer to the procedure as 'bagging' and he told the solicitor about it as soon as he saw him. Despite this, he was charged with robbery and manslaughter and when he came to trial was found guilty and sentenced to twenty years imprisonment.

By itself, the allegation made by Keith Twitchell might have been some fantasy dreamed up to discredit the police: that was certainly what the police claimed and the courts at first believed. However, other victims of torture gradually came to light, men such as Derek Treadaway, who was also arrested by the West Midlands Serious Crime Squad in 1982 and subjected to the same treatment of being handcuffed to a chair and nearly suffocated in order to persuade him to sign an incriminating statement.

Preventing a man from having air until he passed out was a favourite technique of torturers in several parts of Europe from the Middle Ages onwards. Usually, it was done with water. A cloth would be inserted into the subject's mouth and water poured onto it. The weight of the water would drag the material into the throat and the person would begin to struggle for air. This method of torture may be seen in Illustration 20. A version of this torture has been used in recent years by American military interrogators. It is known colloquially as 'waterboarding'. The sensation of being unable to breathe is a terrifying one for most of us and having once experienced it, most of us would do literally anything to avoid repeating the exercise. For the police in the West Midlands 'bagging' had another great advantage: besides being a great way to persuade hard men to sign incriminating statements. It left no visible marks. Burning people with cigarettes and knocking them round the head with truncheons is apt to make people look as though they've been in the wars. This has in the past been the object of unfavourable remark when men have appeared in court after being questioned. It was the dreadful appearance of the men accused of the Birmingham bombings which led to accusations of ill-treatment. With 'bagging', there was nothing to show that anything unorthodox has taken place.

It took many years, but in 1999, the Appeal Court accepted that the accounts of men like Keith Twitchell and Derek Treadaway were quite accurate and that they had been tortured in police stations. Their convictions were overturned and they were awarded compensation for the terrible ordeals which they had undergone. By implication, the court accepted that torture had been carried out by the British police as late as the 1980s.

We must remind ourselves that we are not dealing here with some historical curiosity, but the actions of police officers less than forty years ago. Torture, for the purpose of forcing people to say what the police wished to hear was being used in England until fifteen years or so before the dawn of the twenty-first century.

We have looked at torture in the twentieth century to make people do or say things, it is time now to examine how causing severe pain to criminals was thought to be one way of deterring them from breaking the law in the future. Just as with torture as an aid to interrogation, this is something which was happening in Britain well within living memory. The last flogging to take place in a British prison was in 1962 and, until the passing of the Criminal Justice Act in 1948, five difference offences could still be punished by the courts by ordering the offender to be whipped with the cat-o'-nine-tails. These were the Treason Act 1842; aggravated robbery, under the Security Against Violence Act 1863, the so-called Garrotters' Act; loitering with intent to commit a felony, contrary to the Vagrancy Act 1824; procuration and living on the earnings of prostitutes, Criminal Law Amendment Act 1912; and slaughtering horses without a license, Knacker's Act 1786. Just think: seventy years ago, one could have been flogged for just hanging around a street at night, looking as though one were up to no good!

In reality of course, beggars and tramps were not being whipped for vagrancy as they sometimes were in the seventeenth and eighteenth centuries. Very occasionally, a suspected person loitering with intent might receive the 'cat', but such cases were vanishingly rare in the twentieth century. That such offences as slaughtering horses without a licence and loitering with intent remained punishable by flogging well into the twentieth century was an anachronism; it was just that nobody ever got around to altering these statutes. The same applied to treason and, by and large, living off immoral earnings. In the 22-year period between 1913 and 1935, just twenty-five men were flogged for this, roughly one a year. The only crime for which flogging was really ordered by courts in the twentieth century was robbery with violence. In the first 35 years of the twentieth century, a total of 466 men were awarded the 'cat' for robbery with violence. The situation was different in prisons, where flogging could be given for various infringements of discipline, but we shall look at that later in this chapter.

During the nineteenth century flogging, as a punishment for crimes committed outside the prison system, fell into disuse. It was revived during the 'Garrotting' panic of the 1860s and from then on carried out almost exclusively against those convicted of robbery with violence. This state of affairs continued until 1948, with only those guilty of this offence facing the prospect of the 'cat'. It was widely believed that the threat of the 'cat' kept violent crime in check during the Edwardian period and the years between the two world wars. In 1954, after both the 'cat' and birch had been abandoned, other than for offences against discipline committed by those serving a prison sentence, a well-known detective wrote an article for the *Daily Mirror*. 'Fabian of the Yard', as he was known, had no doubt at all about the benefit to society of retaining the ability to flog violent criminals. In his article he explained, quite correctly, that once a man had been flogged with a cat-o'-nine-tails, he took great care not to run the risk of ending up being whipped a second time. Fabian thought that this fear of pain was a healthy one, that could protect society from hooligans and dangerous men. He was keen to see that its use in prisons was not removed, as he felt that it was the only thing which kept prison warders safe from attack. Fabian wrote:

Prison doesn't worry such men. And how can we judge by normal human standards a man who is not worried by prison? Gaol is a rotten place. It is a hell-hole, don't mistake me. Yet these men don't fear it. What then do they fear? Only that one thing. The 'cat.'

Yes, I know this kind of talk is out of date. And I realize that prison floggings will also one day be out of date, just as prisons will be. I shall be glad to see that day when in some distant tomorrow we understand criminals well enough to cure them.

But right now we have not reached such a stage. We still have prisons and in them we keep dangerous men. While these men exist the 'cat' must stay. And it must be used. It is the only protection prison officers have.

Fabian went on to tell an anecdote of his time at a London police station, which he claimed indicated clearly the deterrent power of the 'cat';

I remember one day while I was an inspector at the old Vine-street police station. It was a Sunday afternoon and a man was brought in charged with jumping out at an elderly woman and trying to steal her handbag in Berkeley- square.

I looked at the thief, who was a real old lag. And then at the woman, who hardly reached up to his elbow, and who looked as frail as a plucked sparrow. 'When he grabbed her handbag, sir,' said the police constable, 'she wouldn't let go. She took hold of his jacket lapels and held on to him until I arrived on the scene, sir. He made some efforts to escape, but was apparently unable to do so.'

I asked the old lady: 'He didn't try to hit you, then, madam?' The thief broke in. 'Hit her, guv? Not me, guv! I don't want my back scratched!'

It was the 'cat' he meant. The 'cat' he feared. And undoubtedly, although the shock and pain must be markedly severe, yet I do not think it is the physical agony that makes judicial corporal punishment so dreaded by these men. It is the disgrace.

Chief Inspector Fabian has been quoted at length, not only to give a flavour of the views of some people at the time on the subject of flogging, but also because he was closely involved with one of the most famous cases during the inter-war years where a criminal trial ended in those convicted being sentenced to the 'cat'. This was the affair of the so-called 'Mayfair Boys', well-to-do young men who had turned to crime after their families had failed to supply them with as much money as they thought they needed.

In 1937, debates were taking place about the usefulness, or otherwise, of the birch and 'cat' as punishment. Many people thought that both implements were horribly outdated and the sooner that they were done away with, the better. Not everybody agreed. The judiciary and police were, by and large, strongly in favour of their retention. Into the midst of this public debate came a shocking case, which involved not young tearaways or hardened criminals, but rather four young men from good families, all of whom had attended public schools.

A week before Christmas 1937, four men in their mid-twenties planned a robbery which would free them from their financial difficulties. They had all grown up with plenty of money, been expensively educated and generally been raised with the feeling that they were superior to the ordinary men and women in the street. They had little inclination to work and their families had gradually withdrawn financial support, until all four of them were short of money. They were typical 'men-about-town' of the period and frequented Mayfair clubs and hotels, chiefly on credit, which was only forthcoming because of their class. However, by the end of 1937, this was wearing a little thin and it was essential that they should have some ready cash. The men concerned were Robert Harley, David Wilmer, Peter Jenkins and Christopher Lonsdale and they ranged in age from 22 to 26.

The scheme which the four men who became popularly known as 'The Mayfair Boys' devised was simplicity itself. This was a time when class and accent meant everything. One of them rang up Cartier, the jewellers, and spoke to Mr Etienne Bellenger, one of the directors. He was told that the caller wished to buy an expensive engagement ring and asked him to bring a selection of nine rings to the Hyde Park Hotel, where he was staying. The hapless Mr Bellenger, doubtless impressed both by the young man's beautiful voice and the fact that he was staying in such an exclusive hotel, duly turned up with nine rings, worth in total over £13,000. Once he was in the hotel room, Bellenger was knocked to the floor by David Wilmer and then savagely beaten by Robert Harley. As a result of the attack, he spent several weeks in hospital. It was later said that he was lucky not to have been killed, so violent was the attack.

It did not take the police very long to track down those responsible for the robbery. Wilmer's fingerprints were found on a bottle and glass in the room where the rings had been stolen. Robert Harley had been working as an informer for the police for several months and tried to turn in his fellow robbers for the reward. The attack on the man from Cartier had made the headlines of all the newspapers and Harley thought that he might make more from the reward than he could get from selling on the stolen jewellery. All four men were arrested and within two months appeared at the Old Bailey before Lord Hewart, the Lord Chief Justice. They were charged with conspiracy and robbery with violence.

As is so often the case, the four defendants relied on what is known in legal circles as a 'cut-throat' defence, in which they all admitted being concerned in the crime, but each tried to lay the blame for the worst aspects on the others. As is usually the end-result in such cases, the jury were unimpressed and convicted them all of conspiracy and three of robbery with violence. Pleas of mitigation were made, which centred around the fact that the men had attended good schools and universities and came from very respectable families. The Lord Chief Justice was scathing about this when passing sentence on 18 February 1938. He said:

> The word 'education' has been used about each of you. If I believed that you really were educated men it would be necessary for me to be, on that account, more severe. Probably all that is meant is that somebody has spent money in providing you with certain conventional opportunities of education. The results are not impressive.

The men in the dock can have had little doubt that they would end up being sent to prison for years for their crime and so it proved. Harley received seven years, Wilmer five, Jenkins three years and Lonsdale, the least culpable of them, was sent to prison for eighteen months. All this was as expected. What came as a shock both to the prisoners and everybody else was that Lord Hewart also ordered that two of the men, those who had actually taken part in the attack on Etienne Bellenger, should also be flogged. Robert Harley was to receive twenty strokes of the 'cat' and David Wilmer fifteen.

There was some disquiet about the idea of these young men from respectable families being flogged, not least because the Cadagon Commission on Corporal Punishment had been deliberating about the future of flogging and was still to deliver its report. Some people thought that it would be wrong to flog these men, when that type of punishment might soon be abolished. The MP for Kirkaldy raised the matter in the House of Commons, asking the Home Secretary if he would consider remitting that part of the sentence relating to the flogging. He also asked when the commission on corporal punishment would issue their report. Other MPs asked similar questions. In the event the two 'Mayfair Boys' were both given the 'cat' before the report on corporal punishment was published in March 1938. As expected, it recommended the complete abolition of both the 'cat' and the birch, except as punishments in prisons, for those attacking warders. A bill was prepared with a view to putting these measures into law, but of course there were so many more urgent considerations to be dealt with at that time, the Second World War began the following year, that these measures did not find their way onto the stature book for another ten years.

The 1948 Criminal Justice Act ended flogging as a penalty available for the courts, although there were many people who were sorry to see the end of this ancient British tradition. The main reason for passing the act which ended centuries of whipping had nothing to do with humanitarian feelings but was simply a question of pragmatism; flogging did not actually deter crime. Violent crime had risen in England in the first thirty-five years of the twentieth century, as it had also done in Scotland. However, in England, where the 'cat' and birch were available to the courts, such crime had risen by 33 per cent, but in Scotland, with no corporal punishment, it had only gone up by 6 per cent.

It was to be another fifteen years before England saw the last of the 'cat' and birch. Their use in prisons declined after the 1948 Act: most thoughtful and liberal people saw flogging as a barbaric relic of an earlier age and it was used very sparingly through the 1950s. Not that it vanished completely. In December 1952, 22-year-old William McGuire was flogged with the 'cat' in Dartmoor Prison, following an attack on a warder. McGuire was given twelve strokes. The following year, a prisoner in Wandsworth was sentenced to eighteen strokes of the 'cat', but for medical reasons, he was instead birched.

By 1960, the use of both the birch and 'cat' was clearly an anachronism in a modern society. Using pain as a means of punishment was no longer acceptable and it was a question of *when* the practice fell into abeyance, rather than *if*. Flogging, like hanging, had had its day. It is in retrospect faintly surprising that both had managed to survive until the 1960s. Every sentence of flogging had to be referred to and confirmed by the Home Secretary, who often withheld his permission. The whole business was becoming an embarrassment and the end came suddenly with a change of government in 1964. Before then, there were to be a handful of final cases of the judicial use of corporal punishment.

The 'cat' was hardly ever ordered after 1953. Instead, the birch was the chosen instrument. In 1962 four adult male prisoners were birched for offences against the prison rules, all entailing violence. The last of these floggings took place on 29 May that year. The victim, who was to become famous a few years later, was 33-year-old Frank Mitchell. Mitchell, who had spent some time in Broadmoor, was nicknamed the 'Mad Axeman', following his exploits during a prison escape when he terrorised a woman by brandishing an axe. On 23 April 1962, Mitchell and half a dozen other prisoners managed to get out of their cells and attacked a prison officer. Frank Mitchell got hold of a truncheon and smashed it so hard across the warder's face that the truncheon snapped in two. For this, he was given fifteen strokes on his bare backside with the birch. This was followed by two weeks on a diet of bread and water. A few years later, the Kray brothers helped Frank Mitchell to escape from prison and then, finding him to be a liability, had him murdered.

Deliberately inflicting pain on men and then starving them by limiting their food and drink to bread and water was really not how civilized societies deal with misbehaviour. That at least was the view of Home Secretaries from 1962 onwards. Henry Brooke, who was appointed Home Secretary three months after Frank Mitchell was birched, refused to authorize any more flogging of any kind, under any circumstances. In March 1963, two prisoners who had assaulted a prison officer at Dartmoor were ordered to be birched, but the Home Secretary refused to sanction the punishment. Instead, he made arrangements for the men to see a psychiatrist, much to the disgust of the Prison Officers' Association.

In October 1964, a general election was held, which was won by Labour. Like Henry Brooke, the new Home Secretary, Frank Soskice, would not allow anybody to birched or flogged with the 'cat', the same approach taken by his successor, Roy Jenkins. In November 1966, a prisoner called Roger Maxwell was awarded the birch, but Roy Jenkins refused to allow it to be administered. The following year, judicial corporal punishment was removed forever from the statute book. The wonder of it is that it managed to hang on for so long.

The debate about flogging continued for some decades after its eventual abolition. Older readers might recall that during the 1960s and 1970s, the cry of 'Bring back the cat!' was raised from time to time, frequently in the aftermath of some especially violent crime. The idea of judicial flogging was kept alive in Britain by the fact that it was still being used in parts of the British Isles until 1976. Reactionaries in England could look to these places, praise the law-abiding nature of their societies and attribute it to the wholesome fear of being beaten if one stepped out of line!

The birch was retained in both the Isle of Man and the Channel Islands long after it had fallen into disuse in mainland Britain. The 1948 law which abolished it in most of Britain, did not apply either to the Isle of Man or the Channel Islands, both of which are Crown Dependencies with their own laws and customs. Not only did the Isle of Man not abandon the birch at the same time as the rest of Britain, in 1960 it actually extended its use, passing the Summary Jurisdiction Act, which made it available to be used against youths up to the age of 21. It proved so effective at stemming the sort of juvenile delinquency seen in mainland Britain that there was no real opposition to its use. Even the British government did not seem to be too worried about the fact that courts in the British Isles were ordering men to be flogged.

The birch, although sometimes regarded as being a milder punishment than the 'cat' was, by all accounts, at least as painful. One person who was birched described the sensation as being akin to having a red-hot poker pressed against the bottom. It must of course be borne in mind that the beating was invariably carried out on the bare bottom, which increased the pain felt substantially. Up to twelve strokes were delivered. Although the Isle of Man was the place which was associated in many British people's minds with the use of the birch, it was actually more commonly given to young men living in the Channel Islands of Jersey and Guernsey. Throughout the 1950s and 1960s, courts in the Channel Islands ordered birchings without anybody on the mainland taking much notice. The focus of attention was always upon the Isle of Man.

A typical example of the kind of offence for which the birch was given on the Isle of Man was seen in 1969. That year, a 16-year-old boy appeared in court at the Manx town of Castletown. He was admitted firing an air pistol at two 15-year-olds, one a boy and the other a girl. For this, he was convicted of two counts of assault. Nor was this all. He was in addition found guilty of fifteen other charges, ranging from buying alcohol for children to causing a breach of the peace. If ever, one might think, a short, sharp shock was called for, this young man would be a prime candidate! This was certainly how the case presented itself to local butcher George Costain, who was the Chair of the Magistrates. He sentenced the youth to receive four strokes of the birch. To those living on the Isle of Man, this seemed quite reasonable and was, they believed, one of the reasons that their part of the British Isles was not plagued with vandalism and hooliganism, in the way that England was.

The specifications for the birch used on the Isle of Man were as follows:

Weight not to exceed 9 oz. Length 40 in. Handle length 15 in. Circumference at centre 6 in. Circumference at butt of handle 3½ in. Circumference 6 in. from end 3-¼in.

The last birching took place on the Isle of Man in 1976, although it was not finally abolished for another seventeen years. This was a direct consequence of the practice having been ruled, at the European Court of Human Rights, to constitute torture. Specifically, a case was brought on behalf of somebody who had been sentenced to be birched there and the punishment was found by the court of human rights to fall into the category of, 'torture' or 'inhuman and degrading treatment or punishment'. Once the Court of Human Rights had ruled that torture was taking place in the British Isles, the government at Westminster leaned on the Isle of Man and flogging came to an abrupt end there.

It will be remembered that the United Kingdom entered the Common Market, now the European Union, in 1973. This meant that some of the things which the nation might have tolerated on its fringes now became a serious embarrassment. Birching was one of those things which the rest of Europe viewed with horror and so, one way or another, it had to come to an end. Of course, the Isle of Man and Channel Islands did not just retain flogging long after the rest of Britain abandoned it, capital punishment too lingered on in those places. Although nobody had been sentenced to death in the rest of Britain since 1964, the death sentence continued to be pronounced in Jersey and the Isle of Man for another thirty years, although the invariable practice was to commute it to life imprisonment. The last death sentence in the Channel Islands was pronounced in 1984; the Isle of Man was even later. On 10 July 1992 a man called Tony Teare heard the judge at the Douglas court say:

> I can only pronounce one sentence. You will be taken to the Isle of Man jail and thence to a place of legal execution and there hanged by the neck until dead.

The following year, both flogging and hanging were removed from the Isle of Man's statute book.

There can be no doubt that joining Europe meant that Britain had to adopt a far stricter position on torture than was previously necessary. This country had a tradition of beating children and this segued seamlessly into the beating of adults and for many people there was little difference. The principle was the same in both schools and the judicial system; if somebody steps too far out of line, they must be given a painful lesson. It is an ancient idea, that retribution should be the foundation stone of a properly-functioning penal system. This might have been the British point of view, but torture, whether by flogging or any other means, was anathema to most people living in post-war Europe.

Some people might feel that calling birching and whipping with the cat-o'-nine-tails cannot really be called torture. In the final chapter of this book, we are going to examine a series of events in which there can be not the slightest doubt that torture was used not as punishment, but to force information out of suspects. This was sanctioned by ministers of the Crown and took place in the 1970s.

Chapter 10

The Five Techniques

Readers will perhaps have noticed that the story of torture, as practised by the British, has so far shown methods of savage barbarism gradually giving way to milder and less harmful ways of punishing men and women or extracting information from them. The rack and the ordeal by hot iron gave way to the whipping post and pillory, which in turn led to the treadmill and simple beating up of prisoners. At one point in the post-war history of the United Kingdom though, this trend was thrown into reverse and some of the more ancient modes of torture re-emerged from the mists of time to find their way back into the modern world. This was a shocking development and one which was for some years hidden from view. It is only in recent years that the full horror of what was being done to suspected criminals, all of whom were technically innocent, by the armed forces and police of the United Kingdom has come to light. Let us take one example of an ancient torture which was for centuries found useful when interrogating prisoners and see how it was used in part of the United Kingdom just forty years ago.

The water torture was popular for centuries in Europe, as a way of persuading people to talk. There were various forms, but most involved no more complicated equipment than a piece of cloth and a jug of water. Here is an account of the torture as it was carried out in the seventeenth century. After the victim was tied securely on his back:

> Besides this, the torturer throws over his mouth and nostrils a thin cloth, so that he is scarcely able to breathe through them, and in the meanwhile a small stream of water like a thread, not drop by drop, falls from on high, upon the mouth of the person lying in this miserable condition, and so easily sinks down the thin cloth to the bottom of his throat, so that there is no possibility of breathing, his mouth being stopped with water and his nostrils with the cloth, so that the poor wretch is in the same agony as persons ready to die, and breathing out their last.

Compare this account from almost 400 years ago with what Irish Prime Minister Jack Lynch told the British Prime Minister Edward Heath in 1972, when they met in London. Mr Lynch raised the question of a number of men who had been tortured by soldiers of the British Army in recent months, one of whom:

Had been forced to lie on his back on the floor, a wet towel had been placed over his head, and water had been poured over it to give him the impression that he would be suffocated.

The two accounts are identical, except that one happened in seventeenth-century Europe, at a time when torture was widely regarded as an essential adjunct to the questioning of a suspected criminal, and the other in the 1970s in a country where the torture of suspects had been declared by a panel of judges to be illegal, 342 years earlier.

The story of the British Army and Royal Ulster Constabulary's behaviour towards those they believed to be members of terrorist groups is shocking. It is a tale of waterboarding, electric shocks and sleep deprivation, all taking place not in the distant past or in some remote dictatorship of South America or East Asia, but well within living memory, less than 400 miles from London. To understand how such things could happen, it will be necessary to examine briefly the background to what are euphemistically referred to as, 'The Troubles', a state of armed conflict in part of the United Kingdom which lasted for the better part of thirty years.

Until less than a century ago, the independent country known today as Ireland was an integral part of the United Kingdom. True, the English had treated it very often as a conquered and subdued nation, but technically it was still an indivisible part of Britain. All this changed during the First World War, in the middle of which was launched the rebellion against English rule which became known as the Easter Uprising. After the fighting which took place in 1916, there was a mood in Ireland which, in retrospect, made independence inevitable. It was a question of when, rather than if this should happen. No country wishes to see part of its territory break away, though: one need only look at the situation in 2017 with the Spanish government in Madrid and the restive province of Catalonia. The British had no intention of surrendering part of their country and so fought a fierce, rear-guard action against the nationalists who were trying to drive them from Ireland.

After the end of the First World War, the British hired many irregular troops who were little more than mercenaries. To this day, a hundred years later, the reputation of these men is still one of ruthlessness and brutality. These auxiliaries, who were known colloquially as the 'Black and Tans', killed and tortured as they pleased, with the encouragement and approval of the government in London. Lord Longford, who came from an aristocratic Anglo-Irish family and was a teenager at the time of the Irish War of Independence, wrote about the kind of things which the Black and Tans had been doing in Ireland and of which he had personal knowledge. He described how they treated captured Republicans, 'cutting out the tongue of one, the nose of another, the heart of another and battering in the skull of a fourth'. This then was the background which led fifty years later to the last case of the British Army using torture on suspects with the permission and full knowledge of the government.

It may seem incredible in the country which has long regarded itself as the home of democracy, but just fifty years ago there were marches and demonstrations in the United Kingdom calling for 'One man, one vote'. These civil rights marches were by Catholics in Northern Ireland, protesting that they had for many years been systematically discriminated against by the Protestants who held power in the province. Voting in local elections was on the basis of a property qualification, which favoured the Protestants, as they were more likely to be home owners. Even worse, there was plural voting, whereby the owners of business had extra votes. The whole electoral system was shamelessly rigged against the Catholic minority.

As discontent spread through Northern Ireland, spurred on by similar protests by black people in the southern states of America, the government of the province decided to crack down. After the use of armed force proved ineffective, the decision was taken to resort to concentration camps to quell the disturbances. The British have of course a genius for euphemism. We saw above that what was in all but name a civil war, was routinely dismissed as 'The Troubles'. So too when it was felt wise to lock up innocent men in concentration camps, it was considered that the process had best not be called by its right name. In 1971, when the rounding up of suspects, who would in some cases be tortured and then held without trial for years, began, it was described as 'the introduction of internment'.

Following the partition of Ireland a few years after the end of the First World War, six of the northern counties became a semi-autonomous province of the United Kingdom. Because of the civil war which was raging in the rest of Ireland, the part which had achieved independence as the Irish Free State, those running Northern Ireland passed a law which gave them the power to do literally anything at all that they wished in order to maintain their control over the part of Ireland which they ruled. This was the Special Powers Act or, to give it its full and correct name, The Civil Authorities (Special Powers) Act (Northern Ireland) 1922. This act was framed so as to allow the authorities to blow up houses, hold people without trial or even flog them if they wished. If those measures were not sufficient, a clause of the act empowered the Minister of Home Affairs in the Northern Irish Government to, 'to take all such steps and issue all such orders as may be necessary for preserving peace and maintaining order'. Here are one or two sections of the act which might perhaps give a flavour of the thing:

8. It shall be lawful for the civil authority and any person duly authorised by him, where for the purposes of this Act it is necessary so to do: (d) To cause any structures or buildings to be destroyed

5. Where after trial by any court a person is convicted of any crime or offence to which this section applies, the court may, in addition to any other such punishment which may be lawfully imposed, order such a person, if male, to be once privately whipped.

The provisions of the Special Powers Act for the destruction of homes, detention without trial and the flogging of those who broke curfews seem to belong to apartheid-era South Africa, rather than the United Kingdom in the 1970s, but there it was. These were the powers which, in 1971, it was decided to use. Barbed-wire fences were built around an old RAF base and it was turned into a makeshift concentration camp for the hundreds of men who were to be held indefinitely without trial. It is what happened to those men when first they were arrested which concerns us in the present instance, because many of them were tortured mercilessly before being sent off to live for years in corrugated-iron Nissen huts which dated from the Second World War.

We looked in some detail at the idea that Magna Carta forbade torture and found that the evidence for such an assertion is scant. That Magna Carta came out against arbitrary imprisonment, on the other hand, is indisputable. Clause 39 could hardly be clearer on this point: 'No free man shall be taken or imprisoned'. . except by the lawful judgement of his peers'. Whatever else was going on at the time that the Special Powers Act was being brought into play at that time, a coach and horses was being driven through Magna Carta.

Before looking closely at the treatment to which some of these detainees were subjected, is it perhaps stretching things a little to call it torture? Actually, there was never at the time any real dispute about what was being done to the men who were being held without trial. The suggestion that torture was being inflicted upon suspects during their interrogation was not being made by a few republican firebrands, but rather by ministers of the British government in London. Merlyn Rees was Secretary of State for Northern Ireland from 1974 to 1976 and then Home Secretary between 1976 and 1979. If anybody knew what was or was not happening in the province during the early 1970s, Rees was the man. In 1977, he wrote:

It is my view (confirmed by Brian Faulkner before his death) that the decision to use methods of torture in Northern Ireland in 1971/72 was taken by Ministers – in particular Lord Carrington, then Secretary of State for Defence.

In other words, not only were prisoners tortured, but this was done not on the authority of some maverick soldier or police officer, but rather on the orders of the British government.

What is surprising about this, the last time that torture was without doubt used against suspects in the United Kingdom as an aid to questioning, is that nobody really made any effort to conceal what was going on. The facts were never in dispute and the only debate was about what words should be chosen to describe the shocking sessions of torture being conducted by the army and police. For example, when stories first emerged, after detention without trial was re-introduced in August 1971, of the brutality used against those being questioned after the army had picked them up, an enquiry was set up by the British government. It was led by civil servant Sir Edmund Compton.

The report of the Compton Committee, which was published on 16 November 1971 was an absolute gem of obfuscation and euphemism. Sir Edmund found plenty of evidence that the allegations floating around were perfectly true and that the British Army were, in effective, running a torture chamber, but did this amount, as many claimed, to 'brutality'? The report of the Compton Committee thought not and their reason is so priceless that it deserves to be quoted in full:

> Where we have concluded physical ill-treatment took place, we are not making a finding of brutality on the part of those who handled these complaints. We consider that brutality is an unhuman or savage form of cruelty, and that cruelty indicates a disposition to inflict suffering, coupled with indifference to, or pleasure in, the victim's pain. We do not think that happened here.

In short, because the soldiers mistreating these prisoners went about the business in a methodical and unemotional fashion, without enjoying what they were doing, there was no brutality!

It has been necessary to go into the background of the events of that summer a little, to put the torture carried out in its proper context, and also to show how those who knew about it were more worried about the terminology being applied than they were about what was actually *done*. What was done to the men picked up in August 1971 and spirited off to a captivity from which there was no appeal and against which, *habeus corpus* had no power?

At 4:30am on 9 August 1971, the army 'lifted' 342 men from across Northern Ireland. Those whom they felt had valuable information were flown by helicopter to the former RAF base of Ballykelly, where the army had established a special interrogation centre. There, they would have a free hand to practise what became known as the 'five techniques' which would, it was hoped, break the spirit of even the most determined Republican. These five techniques were deprivation of sleep, the withholding of food and drink, constant exposure to 'white noise', hooding and being made to stand against walls for protracted periods of time in stressful and uncomfortable positions. Combined with being beaten and generally knocked about, this sensory deprivation was often sufficient in itself to cause those subjected to it to become disoriented and even to begin suffering from hallucinations.

To begin with, the men would be kept handcuffed and hooded in cold cells. White noise, a constant, loud hissing, prevented them from hearing what was going on around them. At any moment, they might be dragged from their cells and forced to stand with their arms above their heads, leaning against a wall in a position which would cause the muscles to ache after a few minutes. If they fell down, they were beaten or had their heads banged against the wall. After a time, they were returned to their cells. Needless to say, while this was going on, there was no opportunity to sleep and no food or drink was provided.

This treatment in itself was precisely similar to the techniques used by both the Spanish Inquisition and Stalin's secret police to soften up suspects and encourage them to start talking. Sometimes, the application of the 'five techniques' was preceded by making the prisoner run the gauntlet between rows of soldiers wielding batons. Or perhaps the man would be blindfolded and then taken for a ride in a helicopter. After a bit, when he had been told that the helicopter was hovering hundreds of feet in the air, the suspect would be hurled out, only to land with a bump. In fact, the helicopter had been only three or four feet from the ground.

All good things, however, come to an end and after the publication of the Compton Committee's report, the word went out from Downing Street that there was to be no more systematic ill-treatment of prisoners carried out in this way. The five techniques were forbidden until further notice. Indeed, Edward Heath, the Prime Minister at that time, made a public pledge that the five techniques would no longer be used by the army. This unwarranted interference in the day-to-day running of the army in Belfast and Londonderry was a bit of a nuisance for a while, but by the spring of the following year, some new schemes had been devised, which it was hoped would not be likely to leave any permanent marks on those questioned. After being made to run the gauntlet and having been beaten up by squads of soldiers, quite a few of the prisoners looked as though they had been in a car crash. Since the government were now being so fussy, something which would not arouse suspicion would have to be used instead.

There is a popular and wholly mistaken belief that the death penalty for murder was abolished in the United Kingdom some time during the 1960s. This was true for England, Scotland and Wales, but not other parts of the British Isles. In 1984, the death sentence was pronounced upon a man in the Channel Islands and as late as 1992, somebody on the Isle of Man was sentenced to hang. These sentences were both commuted to life imprisonment, as was the last death sentence to be given in Northern Ireland. The story of Liam Holden, the last man to receive a sentence of death in the province is a curious one and shows what the army were up to as soon as they were ordered to stop the systematic torture of arrested Republicans.

On 19 April 1973, 19-year-old Liam Holden was sentenced to death in Belfast for the murder of a British soldier. His sentence was commuted to life imprisonment and he was not released for seventeen years. Some years after he left prison, Holden approached the Criminal Cases Review Commission, which investigates miscarriages of justice in Northern Ireland. In June 2012, Holden's appeal against his conviction was successful, the Crown having decided not to oppose the appeal. It was ruled that Liam Holden's interrogation, which had led to his making a confession, had been carried out unlawfully. By implication, the court accepted that Holden had been questioned in the manner which he described, the details of which are truly horrifying.

After the teenage chef had been picked up by the army, in October 1972, he was taken to the headquarters of the Parachute Regiment's intelligence section. There, according to his own account:

> Six soldiers came into the cubicle where I was being held and grabbed me. They held me down on the floor and one of them placed a towel over my face, and they got water and they started pouring the water through the towel all round my face, very slowly. After a while you can't get your breath but you still try to get your breath, so when you were trying to breathe in through your mouth you are sucking the water in, and if you try to breathe in through your nose, you are sniffing the water in. It was continual, a slow process, and at the end of it you basically feel like you are suffocating

Of course, today we are familiar with this technique and know if by the American expression of 'waterboarding', but it had already been in use centuries before the British Army adopted it in Northern Ireland. Illustration 20, at which we looked in the last chapter, shows waterboarding taking place in medieval Europe. Some things never change and with something as simple as this, needing only a bucket of water and a piece of cloth, there is little wonder that the old water torture is still going strong to this very day. Of course, there is one very great advantage to questioning people in this terrible way and that is that it leaves no marks at all upon the subject. After Liam Holden had been waterboarded for a few hours, an army medic examined him and reported that there were no visible cuts, bruises or other marks on his body.

It is not perhaps surprising that when the water torture was followed up by a threat to shoot the young man and dump his body in a field, he gave in and signed a statement admitting that he had committed murder.

Although nobody at that time used the expression 'waterboarding', the method was used not only by the army, but also by the Royal Ulster Constabulary. It was simple and devastatingly effective. It has been alleged that electric shocks were also used during the interrogation of prisoners at this time, although the evidence for this is somewhat sketchy. What has become apparent in recent years is that the waterboarding of Republican prisoners was no haphazard and improvised business. Men who trained as officers with, for instance, the Royal Marines in the 1960s have testified that as part of their training to withstand questioning of captured by enemy forces, they were waterboarded in precisely the way that the Irish prisoners claimed. In other words, use of the water torture was an accepted practice in the British Army years before Liam Holden's arrest.

The government of the Irish Republic was shocked by the stories emerging from Northern Ireland and took their concerns to the European Commission of Human Rights at Strasbourg. When the case of Ireland v United Kingdom was heard in 1976, the European Commission ruled that what had been done in 1971 and 1972 amounted to torture. Specifically, they said that;

> The systematic application of the techniques for the purpose of inducing
> a person to give information shows a clear resemblance to those methods
> of systematic torture which have been known over the ages

They went on to describe the 'five techniques' as a modern system of torture.

Following an appeal against this ruling, the case was heard in 1978 at the European Court of Human Rights. This led to a revised judgement that the treatment meted out to the detainees did not amount to torture; it was merely inhumane and degrading.

It is a little staggering that less than thirty years before the dawn of the twenty-first century, British troops should, with the connivance of the government in London, have been subjecting men who were never to be brought before the courts to a type of torture which had been popular in the seventeenth century! This, nevertheless, was the position when the water torture was being carried out in part of the United Kingdom in the 1970s. It was, with the exception of the occasional 'beating-up' in English police stations, the last case of torture being used in Britain.

We have traced the history of torture in Britain from the time of the Anglo-Saxons until a few decades before the millennium. In the final section, we shall look at the situation today, a time when the judicial use of torture is not only unthinkable in this country, but is frowned upon to such an extent that the British will not deport anybody to any country where they might be exposed to the possibility of being tortured.

Endword

We have examined the history of torture in Britain and British overseas possession, from the trial by ordeal of the medieval period all the way through to the treatment of suspected criminals in England during the 1980s. Not all the practices at which we have looked are always regarded as torture, in the traditional meaning of the word. However, once we abandoned the word and looked instead at the nature of what was done, which was the judicial infliction of severe pain, it was found that torture has been an enduring theme which runs through almost the whole of British history.

Like most countries in the Western World, the United Kingdom now utterly rejects the use of torture and has signed various treaties and agreements, pledging to have nothing to do with the practice. This attitude has become even more fixed since joining the Common Market in 1973. It is an accepted tenet of European civilization today that torture has no place in the judicial or penal system of any nation belonging to the European Union. Of course, Britain had already renounced the use of torture twenty years before becoming a member of the Common Market when it became signatory of the European Convention on Human Rights in the 1950s. This protocol forbids absolutely the use of torture by anybody anywhere in Europe. Indeed, it goes much further than that! Looking at a fairly recent example of a court case which hinged around the use of torture which might not even have happened and even if it had, would have been in another continent, will show us just how scrupulous we have now become about this subject.

Britain, along with most other European countries, refuses to extradite or deport people to countries where they might be executed or tortured. In other words, it is not merely that the British are determined that nobody in their own country shall be tortured, they will also ensure that no action of theirs will put anybody at hazard of being tortured in any other part of the world. This commitment is far-ranging and absolute, being based in part upon a feeling of natural justice and also on Britain's obligations as a signatory to the European Convention on Human Rights. Sometimes, this almost fanatical desire to ensure that nobody is tortured anywhere in the world can have what appear to the unbiased observer to be almost farcical consequences.

In 1993, a Jordanian national arrived in the United Kingdom on a forged passport. The following year this man, a Palestinian called Omar Othman, was granted asylum on the grounds that he faced religious persecution if he returned to his own country. Omar Othman, who is a Muslim cleric, is more commonly known today by his *nom de guerre*, which is Abu Qatada and once he had settled in the United Kingdom, it became apparent that he was actually a very dangerous person indeed. He has been described as Osama Bin-Laden's right-hand man in Europe and copies of his sermons were found in a flat which had formerly been occupied by some of the 9/11 attackers. Before that, in 1999, he had been convicted by a court in Jordan, in his absence, of conspiracy to carry out terrorist attacks. For this, he had been sentenced to life imprisonment with hard labour. In October that year, he delivered a sermon at Finsbury Park mosque in London, in which he called for attacks on English, Jewish and American people.

Following the 2001 attacks on the Pentagon and World Trade Center, to which Abu Qatada had at least some connection, the British government decided that here was a person without whom they could definitely do in their country. He had entered Britain illegally, on a forged passport, he was inciting terrorism here and not only that, the British state was supporting his family to the tune of £800 a week in state benefits! Surely, if ever it was time to call a halt to British hospitality, this was it.

In 2001, Abu Qatada was arrested in connection with terrorism. In 2002, he was arrested again. He was released on bail in 2005 and then rearrested the same year. Proceedings were started with a view to having him removed from the country by deporting him to Jordan, where, it will be recalled, he had already been convicted of a terrorist offence. It was at this point that the attempt struck a huge rock. Well, two rocks, to be precise. One problem was that torture was being pretty freely used in Jordan and even if the British had been prepared to let Abu Qatada run the risk of being tortured, their hands were tied. Britain was a signatory to the UN Convention on Torture, which forbids any of the states who have signed up to the convention from any complicity in torture, not only in their own country, but anywhere else in the world. This was a problem, but not an insurmountable one. Britain sought and received assurances from Jordan that Abu Qatada would not be tortured there.

There was another snag, which was that the European Court of Human Rights, involved in seeing that member states abide by the European Convention on Human Rights, were concerned that evidence obtained by the use of torture against *other* people might be presented if Abu Qatada was to appear in a Jordanian court. The saga dragged on until 2013, until the British government succeeded in getting assurances from the Jordanians that no evidence tainted by torture would be used against Abu Qatada, who was finally put on an RAF plane and delivered back to Jordan, where the case against him promptly collapsed and he was freed!

This one case has been studied in some detail to illustrate just how fantastically cautious Britain is today to make quite sure that not only is nobody tortured in Britain itself, but that nobody should face torture anywhere else in the world either. This state of affairs is unlikely ever to change, even after Britain has withdrawn from the European Union. Leaving Europe will not mean that Britain reneges on its commitment to the European Convention on Human Rights, which is entirely separate from the laws of the European Union. Nor is Britain likely at any time in the future to renounce the UN Convention on Torture, which also binds signatory countries to certain standards, not only in their own territories, but when having dealings with any other nation.

Gazing into and predicting the future is a chancy and uncertain business, but as far as it is possible to say anything definite about the future conduct of any nation, we can be pretty sure that Britain has finished with its long tradition of using torture for good and all, something in which all right-thinking men and women will rejoice. It might be said though, that our legacy lived on, even after the liquidation of the British Empire. We looked earlier in detail at the history of Britain's use of torture in India and saw that it lasted for the better part of 200 years. The torture was of course carried out mostly by Indians themselves, acting on behalf of their British masters and despite various enquiries and commissions, mistreating and abusing suspects went on right up to 1948, when the country was granted independence. This was not the end of the torture though.

On 4 November 1976, almost thirty years after the British left, a man called Hirman Laxman Pagar was arrested by the police in the Indian state of Andhra Pradesh. According to his statement, Pagar was stripped naked and a long stick, coated with chilli powder, was pushed up his anus, a trick that we saw being used in India in the nineteenth century. By all accounts, the use of chilli powder as an aid to interrogation is still popular with the Indian police to this day. Colonialism has cast a very long shadow in the country.

Of one thing we may be very glad and that is that torture is now viewed as such a strange and undesirable aberration, that the chances of its ever being used again by the British or their agents is vanishingly small, something which we probably all agree is an improvement on the way things were even a few decades ago.

Bibliography

Abbot, Geoffrey, *Rack, Rope and Red-hot Pincers: A History of Torture and Its Instruments*, London, Brockhampton Press, 1993.

Abbot, Geoffrey, *Torture: Persuasion at its Most Gruesome*, Chichester, Summersdale Publishers, 2016

Andrews, William, *Medieval Punishments: An Illustrated History of Torture*, New York, Skyhorse Publishing, 2013.

Arlidge, Anthony, and Judge, Igor, *Magna Carta Uncovered*, Oxford, Hart Publishing, 2014.

Brandon, David, and Brooke, Alan, *London: The Executioner's City*, Stroud, Sutton Publishing, 2006.

Briggs, Asa, *A Social History of England*, New York, The Viking Press, 1983.

Cobain, Ian, *Cruel Britannia: A Secret History of Torture*, London, Portobello Books, 2013.

Donnely, Mark P., and Diehl, Daniel, *The Big Book of Pain; Torture and Punishment through History*, Stroud, The History Press, 2008.

Elkins, Caroline, *Britain's Gulag: The Brutal End of Empire in Kenya*, London, Johnathon Cape, 2005.

Everett, Suzanne, *History of Slavery*, London, Grange Books, 1996.

Fraser, Antonia, *The Gunpowder Plot: Terror and Faith in 1605*, London, Weidenfeld & Nicolson, 1996.

French, David, *Fighting EOKA: The British Counter-Insurgency Campaign on Cyprus, 1955-1959*, Oxford, Oxford University Press, 2015.

Green, Johnathon, *Famous Last Words*, London, Omnibus Press, 1979.

Grose, Francis, *Military Antiquities Respecting a History of the English Army, from the Conquest to the Present Time*, London, S. Hooper, 1786.

Innes, Brian, *The History of Torture*, London, Brown Packaging Books, 1998.

Jones, Steve, *Capital Punishments; Crime and Prison Conditions in Victorian Times*, Nottingham, Wicked Publications, 1992.

Kellaway, Jean, *The History of Torture and Execution: From Early Civilisation Through Medieval Times to the Present*, London, Mercury Books, 2003.

Kerrigan, Michael, *The Instruments of Torture*, Staplehurst, Spellmount Publishers, 2000.

Lewis, Geoffrey, *Behind the Walls: A Chelmsford Turnkey of the Nineteenth Century*, Biggleswade, Watkiss Studios, 1996.

Marshall, Henry, *The Recruiting of the Army, Military Punishments*, London, John Murray, 1846.

Murphy, Michale, Joseph, *Fiendish Ingenuity: An Illustrated History of Torture Through the Ages*, Createspace Independent Publishing Platform, 2010.

O'Mara, Shane, *Why Torture Doesn't Work: The Neuroscience of Interrogation*, Massachusetts, Harvard University Press, 2015.

Peters, Edward, *Torture*, Pennsylvania, University of Pennsylvania Press, 1996.

Samuel, E., *An Historical Account of the British Army and the Law Military*, London, Clowes, 1816.

Scott, George Ryley, *A History of Torture Throughout the Ages*, London, Luxor Press, 1940.

Seddon, Peter, *The Law's Strangest Cases*, London, Portico, 2005.

Slee, Christopher, *The Guinness Book of Lasts*, Enfield, Guinness Publishing, 1994.

Thompson, Irene, *The A to Z of Punishment and Torture: From Amputation to Zero Tolerance*, Kibworth, Book Guild Publishing, 2008.

Vernon, Jack, *The Illustrated History of Torture*, London, Carlton Publishing Group, 2011.

Webb, Simon, *Execution: A History of Capital Punishment in Britain*, Stroud, The History Press, 2011.

Webb, Simon, *Bombers, Rioters and Police Killers: Violent Crime and Disorder in Victorian Britain*, Barnsley, Pen & Sword Books, 2015.

Wisnewski, Jeremy, *The Ethics of Torture*, London, Continuum, 2009.

Index